Chris Leonard has written for both children and adults – mainly biographies and devotional works. This is her fifteenth published book. She contributes regular Bible-reading notes and also enjoys leading creative-writing courses and holidays. Her writing and teaching spring from lifelong faith, love of drawing out all the good things that are in people, and a degree in English and theology. She is married with two grown-up children and lives in Surrey. Her website is at www.chris-leonard-writing.co.uk.

LEANING TOWARDS EASTER

Readings and stories from
Ash Wednesday to Easter Monday

Chris Leonard

First published in Great Britain in 2005

Society for Promoting Christian Knowledge
36 Causton Street
London SW1P 4ST

British Library Cataloguing-in-Publication Data
A catalogue record for this book is available from the British Library

ISBN 0–281–05612–9

1 3 5 7 9 10 8 6 4 2

Typeset by Graphicraft Ltd, Hong Kong
Printed in Great Britain by Bookmarque Ltd, Croydon, Surrey

*This book is dedicated to
all the quiet but amazing people
who have a story of hope to tell*

Contents

Acknowledgements

———•◆•———

I would like to thank the following people for permission to include pieces of their own writing which appear on the pages indicated:

Jennifer Louis for 'No sweets for Lent', on page xi, 'Time that washes out' on page 34 and 'When a candle burns' on pages 33–4
Fiona Veitch Smith, page 3
Dr Jenny Watts, pages 5–6
William Hipkin for the poem 'Adolescent fumblings' and related story on pages 14–15
Margaret Burtenshaw, page 23
Debra Elsdon for the story on pages 28–9 and the poem 'Hand signals' on pages 27–8
Simon Lord, pages 36–7
Richard Narain, pages 44–5
Mary Huggins, pages 48–50
Judy Yates, pages 54–6
Marina for the poem 'In the night' on pages 58–9
Morag Bramwell, page 61
Susan Holt for the poem 'Stirring' on pages 63–4
Margaret Dean, page 66
Steve Elmes, pages 68–9
Lucy-May Johnson, pages 74–5
Inger Barnes for the poem 'Majesty' on pages 91–2
Val Ramsay, pages 102–3
Edna Cole, page 105

Acknowledgements

Sue Varley, pages 110–11
Angela Griffiths, pages 120–1
Pam Conolly for the poem 'The kiss' on pages 128–9
Caroline Lovejoy, pages 131–2
Kate Davonport, pages 137–9

Other stories have been written up by the author, in the first or third person. Thank you, everyone, for telling them to her, giving permission to use them and for checking their accuracy. Unattributed poems are by the author.

Scripture quotations are taken from the HOLY BIBLE, NEW INTERNATIONAL VERSION. Copyright © 1973, 1978, 1984 by International Bible Society. Used by permission of Hodder & Stoughton Ltd, a member of the Hodder Headline Plc Group.

Introduction

Lent – what is it about, what's it for? Giving things up? Perhaps. Winter seasons, where most things are stripped away, seem part of God's design; and yet even winters have laughter and sledge-tumbles and sparkling, startling beauty. A woman called Jennifer Louis showed me a poem she wrote in Moscow. A thaw had begun during the Lent after her husband's death, and grief heightened her craving for sweet things. For me her words highlight the way God brings delightful, sometimes extravagant, surprises, just when we think it appropriate to be sombre.

> No sweets for Lent,
> no sugar things –
> it's not so hard
> to keep away from tastings.
> But what a surprise
> when Nature spreads the ground
> with her own teasing
> kind of coconut ice!
> It's crunchy-soft, translucent,
> opalescent white,
> and breaks in chunks
> just like it should,
> except it's only white.
> No raspberry colour here,
> no taste, no smell
> of coconut so nice,
> just sound and sight and feel
> of – coconut ice.

Is Lent about meditating on Christ's sufferings and our sin so as to reach a place of repentance? Partly. But what bothers me is that when we finally reach Easter – the astounding miracle of resurrection with its promise of new, transformed life – we celebrate for merely a day or two. Of course we need to recognize that, without Jesus' suffering, and our suffering with him, grace would be so cheap as to be almost worthless. And yet if he had not been raised from the dead our hope would be in vain. Sometimes it feels as though we spent for ever gathering ourselves, crouching for a huge leap and then, having soared, fail to take the time to understand that we have landed somewhere entirely different.

So, this Lent and Easter, come with me on a journey through salvation history to explore that special place of resurrection hope. This newness of life and freedom which Christ's death and resurrection usher in – what difference does it make in the lives of ordinary Christians today? What is the hope, the good news, embodied in the whole story of Jesus' life on earth? I find it expressed most clearly at the start of Christ's earthly ministry when, in his home synagogue, he read the passage from Isaiah 61, then made the startling announcement that, 'Today this scripture is fulfilled in your hearing' (Luke 4.16–21). That's why I've chosen themes for each week or part-week based on the hope expressed in Isaiah 61: for example, that Christ will turn darkness to light, oppression to freedom, not just for individuals but for the world.

Easter speaks of a new hope. Yet we haven't entered it fully. Darkness remains in our world and in our lives, along with oppression, grief and all the rest. I don't know about you but I find Christian books full of mega-miracle-a-minute stories depressing. Maybe I'm doing something wrong, but my life isn't like that. Yet ask any 'ordinary', even not-very-good Christian and, in my experience, every one is able to give a 'reason for the hope that they have' (1 Peter 3.15). Those reasons will be based on what Christ did over 2,000 years ago – but Easter means he's still alive, so I asked individuals how they have found hope amid their everyday circumstances. I asked for small, plain realities, not 'sock-it-to-'em, happy-ever-after' extravaganzas. In my own experience, during dark times, the Holy Spirit often brings hope in little ways – brief shafts of light, quiet words of encouragement, unexpected peace in a tumultuous moment.

> With dark leaves, majestic trees
> drink summer's light.
> But not now!
> Time for frail primroses
> to star the forest floor,
> sparking joy
> for those with eyes to see.

I'd like to thank everyone who has been so honest in allowing me to use their stories of hope for this book. In some sensitive instances names have been changed but otherwise everything is true. Through their stories evidence accumulates that Easter hope still shines today – and don't we need it? Not all of the people whose stories are in this book would call themselves Christians, but why would God restrict giving hope to believers? Hope is so much part of his nature and, along with faith and love, shines as one of the three things which will endure.

Finally, for one day of each week, I've put myself into the shoes of a character in the biblical accounts of Jesus' death and resurrection and written him, or her, an imaginary monologue.

So, what does Lent mean to me? The word itself comes from the Old English for 'springtime'. But to me it also suggests leaning – leaning on God, leaning towards Easter.

Beauty from ashes

Ash Wednesday

[Jesus] took the cup, gave thanks and offered it to them, saying,
'Drink from it, all of you. This is my blood of the covenant,
which is poured out for many for the forgiveness of sins. I
tell you, I will not drink of this fruit of the vine from now on
until that day when I drink it anew with you in my Father's
kingdom.'   (Matthew 26.27–9)

So, this is the start of Lent. I wonder what Ash Wednesday
means to you? For many it means deciding what to give up:
chocolate, alcohol, television, meat . . . For some, since the time
of Charlemagne in the ninth century, it has meant the start of
a 40-day fast. Doctors say that's the most a strong adult should
undertake, without risking permanent damage. It echoes the
wilderness fast at the start of Christ's ministry, with overtones
of spiritual battles, of temptations resisted and pleasant ways
denied.

The junior day school I attended was run by nuns. On Ash
Wednesday the Roman Catholic girls would troop off to the
church round the corner in what would have been first lesson
of the morning, returning with dirty faces. Our teachers, especially solemn, explained that the priest dipped his finger in
ashes preserved from the burning of last year's Palm Sunday
branches. Then he marked each forehead with a cross, saying,
'Remember, O man, that dust thou art and unto dust thou
shalt return.' The weight of his reminder that the girls should
grieve over their sin and prepare for a holy death cast a shadow

1

over our games of jacks or skipping at break. We didn't even consider playing the forbidden 'British Bulldog, one, two, three'. By lunchtime the ashen marks had all but disappeared and we'd largely forgotten – though some did boast about what they were giving up for Lent and I remember learning a great deal about 'Our Lord's Sufferings' at that school.

At the other extreme Lent suggests springtime – the Old English word 'Lencten' means 'spring'. From the short, dark days of January, as we look forward to spring and count down to what used to be the pagan fertility festival of Easter, succulent green bulb-buds start pushing fatly through brown earth, then paint the drabbest urban spaces with white, orange, yellow and rich purple. New life and hope follow the death-throes of winter: Ash Wednesday reminds me of the legend of the phoenix rising from the ashes of its own funeral pyre; or of how some tree seeds are released only by the heat of a forest fire and germinate best in the rich minerals of their parents' ashes. These are not just pagan symbols of new life. They remind us that Jesus' suffering and death would have achieved little had his resurrection not followed, blasting a way through death. Today he offers us an entirely new quality of life. Eternal life can be ours here and now, in so far as we accept his power to love one another as he loves us.

Ash Wednesday, Lent – and Easter – mean many things. Above all, to me they mean a real and costly hope. To think of Lent in terms of leaning towards Easter may have no basis in theology or word derivations, but it's certainly a good direction in which to lean!

* * *

Young journalist Fiona Veitch Smith writes here of how the start of Lent has assumed a special meaning for her.

Today is Ash Wednesday, the day my unborn baby was cremated. The miscarriage took place six weeks ago when my baby was 13 weeks old. I have cried many tears since that day and tossed an equal number of questions at God. 'Why didn't you tell me this was going to happen?' was most often on my lips. As a Christian, I somehow expected that he would let me know if something terrible was going to happen. But he didn't.

I look back in my journal and read the prayer I prayed when I first started bleeding: 'The bleeding got heavier today and I'm more concerned that it's a miscarriage. But you say not to worry, that the baby is fine. Oh Lord, I don't want to lose this baby.'

And God's answer, what I heard him say in my heart, was: 'Be at peace, my child. My angels are surrounding you. I love you, I love your husband Rod and I love the baby. Be at peace.'

Two days later I was in hospital having my dead child removed. I felt betrayed; I felt that God had lied to me. But as I prayed over the next days and weeks I saw that God hadn't lied. The baby is fine; the baby is alive, just not here with me on earth. What irritated me was people saying that my child was now a little angel with Jesus, that he'd be a baby for ever. That was the saddest thing I could imagine: my baby never growing, always being 13 weeks old and never achieving his potential. That was cold comfort.

But again, through talking to God and listening to his voice in my heart, I now believe that my baby, whom I've called Benjamin, will continue to grow in heaven and be all that the Lord created him to be. That is the hope that God has put in my heart, the hope that every Easter will now remind me of: death is not the end of life, it is the beginning of a new one. And because Jesus rose from the grave, I know with all certainty that I will see Benjamin again some day.

You might like to review the familiar words of today's reading with an imaginative eye. What did Jesus' disciples feel like? They'd met for a Passover meal, to celebrate God's deliverance of his people from slavery in Egypt to begin a new life. Imagine their horrified reaction when, before they drank the special wine, Jesus told them it was his blood. At 33, he was very much alive. They knew that he'd put himself in danger by coming to Jerusalem. He'd told them he was about to die, betrayed by one of them. They couldn't understand why, let alone how, he would be alive and drinking the wine 'new with them in my Father's kingdom'. Let your imagination turn to worship. He has brought life from death, so we can eat that bread and drink that wine in his Kingdom.

Thursday

[The LORD has anointed me . . .]
to comfort all who mourn, and provide for those who grieve
   in Zion –
to bestow on them a crown of beauty
instead of ashes,
the oil of gladness
instead of mourning,
and a garment of praise
instead of a spirit of despair.
They will be called oaks of righteousness, a planting of the LORD
for the display of his splendour.

(Isaiah 61.2c–3)

'A crown of beauty instead of ashes' also expresses part of what Lent and Easter mean to me. The theme of ashes appears throughout God's dealings with humankind. Isaiah refers here to huge destruction and suffering as much of Judah was carted into exile. God intended this not as a vindictive punishment for the people's prolonged rebellion against him, but as a way to draw them back to him, to help them repent. God is more hurt by the break in the relationship than any parent could be by a beloved child. Isaiah prophesies how God will replace their misery with comfort and restoration.

Who would have thought, centuries later, that a crown of thorns, delivered to the King of kings with physical cruelty and moral mockery, could become beautiful? Then think of the bleakness of the first Easter Saturday when all the disciples' hopes had turned to bitter ash hot enough to burn. As they ran away to hide, which of them could have imagined that soon they'd be overflowing with praise? Weak, frightened, bewildered – who would have imagined how they would soon be unlocked from despair, and become known as strong pillars, 'oaks of righteousness' for the new 'People of the Way'? That millions all over this world, 20 centuries on, would look at their lives and see God's splendour, see them helping God repair the spiritual devastation of generations?

* * *

God of the big picture and small details, he still delights to bring beauty from ashes. Psychologist and counsellor Dr Jenny Watts told me this story.

> When in mid-November 1999 a fire damaged my house, I did not realize how it would transform my home, life and relationship with God.
>
> I had awoken early in the morning to the smell of burning and, on going downstairs, discovered that the boiler had caught fire in the through-lounge. After I'd turned off the domestic supplies and called the emergency services, an army of engineers, contractors and insurance adjusters descended on me. I was asked to stack any undamaged personal belongings and furniture in the upstairs rooms. It took all day. That night I sank into bed in a very cold house totally exhausted, and prayed that God would sustain me through this crisis.
>
> The next morning I surveyed the damage to the lounge. It felt cold and empty, stripped of everything which had been my home. I could smell and taste soot and everywhere I walked I trod on

debris. Then, as I started to pray, a picture of a new lounge and dining-room came into my thoughts. I advised my insurers, who requested estimates for the additional structural work. Once approved, the refurbishment programme started.

As the house was gradually being restored into a new home, I arranged my commitments around showering at my golf club and eating out. During my evening Bible reading and prayer times, God drew close to me. My eyes were opened and I got to know him in a deeper way. Although my finances took a heavy tumble, he showed me that I could raise the necessary money for the building work and new furniture by selling unwanted items. Two years later I felt that, like my home, I had become 'a new creation'.

Think about times when your life seemed reduced to ashes – from which God later brought forth unexpected beauty. You might like to meditate on 2 Corinthians 5.17: 'Therefore, if anyone is in Christ, he is a new creation; the old has gone, the new has come!'

> from the silence
> music – and a thousand golden
> butterflies rise up

Friday

'I tell you the truth, unless an ear of wheat falls to the ground and dies, it remains only a single seed. But if it dies, it produces many seeds. The man who loves his life will lose it, while the man who hates his life in this world will keep it for eternal life.'
(John 12.24–5)

Many of the important things in my life have come through a kind of death. One example happened after university. In my early twenties I found the beginnings of a career and a new home in a different part of the country. I found a lively new church where I felt cared for and could grow and the beginnings of a relationship with the man who was to become my husband. Then I fell ill. A bad cough settled into post-viral fatigue and, after weeks of struggling and trying to get back to work, I returned home so my parents could 'look after me'. I wasn't even near dying, but it felt as though many of the things I cared about were. I felt irritable and wasn't the best of company, but John phoned me every night and drove all the way to see me as often as he could. He saw me at my worst – and still loved me. Looking back, it made a firm foundation for our marriage.

Later I knew that God was urging me to write a book about James, a man in his eighties who had founded the fastest growing church in West Africa. I believe it was God because, although I'd wanted as a child to be a writer, I certainly didn't want to write this book, then. I knew nothing about Africa. I was still breast-feeding and couldn't leave my children to go and interview James. However, his story filled my thoughts until I had to do something about it. The problem appeared solved when someone offered to tape James' answers to my questions – then at least I could get something of his story on paper. Except that he refused to talk, saying he'd 'done nothing'. So the project died and I forgot about it until a year later when a younger missionary friend of his phoned me and said, 'How soon can you fly out to James' retirement home in Northern Ireland? He's happy to talk to you now.' By that time I could leave my children for a few days, meet him and talk with the missionary who had worked alongside him. Later I spent three weeks researching in Ghana, caught the 'writing bug' which has shaped my life ever since – and an amazing church had its history recorded.

I've given trivial examples. Some Christians do literally die for their faith. Early missionaries to that part of Africa known as the 'white man's grave' lasted an average of six months before succumbing to some tropical disease, but that didn't stop more coming. And today Sunday mornings see the worst traffic jams in Ghana because so many are travelling to various churches, demonstrating that 'dead seeds' have borne fruit by the hundreds of thousands.

* * *

Martin Clements told me how his marriage died – and came to a vibrant new life. He married Joanna in 1991. Neither were Christians at the time though Martin, the youngest of eight, thought most of his siblings were 'religious'. Martin and Joanna were interested primarily in earning lots of money so they could buy things. They worked all hours and, though their marriage appeared to be fine for the first year, they didn't spend much time together, nor did children feature in their plans. Then Joanna became pregnant and developed pre-eclampsia. Born prematurely by emergency Caesarean their son Toby couldn't breathe on his own. He needed intensive care for a month in hospital and Joanna took a while to recover too. Meanwhile Martin's business was declared bankrupt. To make ends meet, Joanna had to return to a London job, with long hours. Even so, they struggled financially and she became unwell.

'I needed to grow up,' said Martin. 'Once, when Joanna had severe gastroenteritis, I left her alone all day – in bed upstairs when the only toilet was downstairs. Toby was sick all over his clothes and I just left them in a smelly heap in the kitchen. No wonder Joanna felt she'd crack up. She and Toby went to stay with her parents.'

Beauty from ashes

Martin moved to a rented flat and his life became bleak. He saw Joanna only on fortnightly visits to Toby. He'd lost his house, possessions, job, wife and almost lost his son. Towards the end of 1995 he needed to see his brother Tim, urgently, on a Sunday evening, 'And I knew where he'd be – in church.' Very gently, Tim allowed Martin to see that the only person who could help him now was God. Martin became a Christian at an Alpha course in early 1996 and soon Joanna began to notice a change in him. They stopped 'slinging mud at each other' and, as she put it, 'The bad things in Martin were rubbed out and the good things polished up.' Joanna even started going to the same church and was amazed how they welcomed her as 'Toby's mum', making her feel part of the church family rather than judged. She became a Christian in early 1997 and by May she and Martin were looking for a house together. 'Joanna had been through so much,' said Martin. 'At her worst time she'd told a counsellor it felt like standing on a high precipice in the dark, convinced she was going to fall. Then God became for her solid ground, something to hold on to – or rather she knew he was holding on to her.' They rediscovered the Bible that Martin's older sister had given them. Originally they'd thought it a weird wedding present but now its words spoke to their situation. Psalm 23 in particular meant a lot to them.

Looking back at the painful time of living apart, Martin said, 'I believe God knew that we each had to change first – change our attitudes – and then our marriage would change.' Two-and-a-half years after they split, Martin and Joanna bought a house and moved in together. 'It felt like getting married again,' said Martin, 'but this time it's so different. When we hit a difficulty I don't rush out to buy flowers, thinking that will solve it. We've both grown up. Our priorities have shifted from material-ism to God and to each other. Our marriage is rich and strong now. We're even able to help other people with similar problems.'

You might like to meditate on Psalm 23.

Saturday

Alive again!

No, I'm not going to tell you what it was like, being dead.

You want to know what being raised felt like? Confusing. I had no idea what was going on. I couldn't see anything. Remember a cloth was wrapped around my whole body, though I didn't understand even that at the time. I heard our friend Jesus call my name and I tried to stumble towards the sound but . . . well, I don't suppose anyone's exactly used to walking in grave-clothes. It felt like . . . being in a dream, or a nightmare. Apart from the smell. I remember thinking that I don't usually smell things in dreams. But the stench of spices was overpowering. There was dust in my nose too – I wanted to sneeze and retch. I couldn't move properly and I couldn't see. Then I felt hands start to unwrap me; and there was this huge roar. I thought, there's a whole crowd of people here. It had been quiet before, eerie. And then everything was a dazzle. The sun hurt my eyes. My sisters were hugging me and crying and laughing.

I felt numb. But everyone wanted to see me, to touch me, to make sure it really was me, they said. Eventually they explained what had happened. Then they wanted to know what it was like, being dead. I couldn't tell them of course. I wanted, how I wanted, time to talk with Jesus, but there was no time. He did come to a feast at our house, where he and I were the centres of attention. I'm not used to that – not really the party type, you see. What with my sisters, Martha and Mary, being so much older than me and each so hospitable in her own way, I've always chosen to stay in the background. Now it seemed everyone wanted a little bit of me – and not all the questioning was friendly. Some of the Pharisees were having such a go at Jesus. They asked their clever, loaded questions of me, too. When I looked in their eyes and saw the hatred there, I almost wished I'd stayed dead.

Some of Jesus' friends weren't too happy about the miracle either. Judas told me that it was far too dangerous for Jesus to be so near the capital at that time. 'You do realize we're only half-an-hour's walk from Jerusalem here,' he snapped, as though I'd never been there.

Judas told me that the whole group of them had been lying low two days' journey away, right out at the edge of the desert. But then, after I died, Jesus was determined to come here. It was Thomas who told the rest of them, 'Let's go with him, that we may die with him.' So brave. So foolish, if you believe Judas. He informed me that raising me from the dead had made the authorities even madder with Jesus. As if I didn't know.

I still felt terrible the next day, when most people were on cloud nine. Jesus borrowed a colt and rode into Jerusalem like a king returning triumphant from battle. All the people who'd come to see me followed him and waved palm branches and shouted, 'Hosanna!' But I thought, 'He's going to die!' And he did – or rather, as you know, he was killed, horribly. And all because of me. Yes, really! I was the last straw. Being raised from the dead attracts far too much of the wrong kind of attention. I'm just a young man, nothing special. He was incredibly special. And he died so that I could live. How do you think that made me feel?

Our friends kept telling us we were in danger too, but my sisters and I couldn't care, to be honest. We'd lost the best friend we'd ever had. We felt more cursed and useless than that wretched fig tree down the road. I truly did wish I'd stayed dead.

And then . . . we heard rumours that he'd risen from his tomb.

Do you know what Lazarus means? It means, 'God has helped'. That's a bit of an understatement, in my case.

11

Do you know that Jesus, the resurrected Jesus I mean, came out to Bethany? He lifted up his hands and blessed us here, blessed all his disciples; and it was from just over there that he was taken up into heaven. This dusty little village has become such a beautiful place! Life is more than worth living – it's amazing.

(Based on John 12.1–7 and Matthew 26.6–13)

'God has helped'. Can you bring to mind times when God has helped you, especially times when he drew beauty from the ashes of your life? With him can you face other things which still need his startling, resurrecting, beautifying touch?

Oppression or betrayal to freedom

First Sunday in Lent

To proclaim freedom for the captives.
(Isaiah 61.1)

Imagine living in first-century Israel. Almost everyone would have seen themselves as captives, not only those slung in prison for criminal or political offences. Subjects of Rome's oppressive regime and taxes, most people were captive to grinding poverty, some literally enslaved. Women and children had even fewer rights and freedoms than men, and Jews suffered in addition the stiflingly detailed demands of their religious laws. Certain kinds of incurable disease – leprosy, haemorrhage, mental illness – held sufferers in a kind of prison-exile, separate from the ones they loved. For all these, hope must have seemed thin indeed.

After the resurrection, Jesus' followers started setting people free, calling on God to deliver them from sickness, paralysis and demons. They demonstrated new ways in which family and society could live together without oppression, as equals, respecting one another and having all things in common. Some were released miraculously from prison cells, but persecution increased too. Many of the new Christians might have been free in spirit but paid the price with their bodies and even their lives. In many countries of the world that hasn't changed. More Christians were killed or imprisoned for their faith in the twentieth century, worldwide, than in all the previous centuries put together. What kind of freedom, then, did Jesus have in mind?

The freedom of those who are willing to lose their lives and physical liberty in order to find it?

* * *

I live in a time and place where people enjoy freedoms which people of Jesus' day couldn't have imagined. And yet there are so many ways in which we may remain captives. William Hipkin writes of a particularly lasting type of oppression and captivity, and of how he has begun to walk more freely.

Adolescent fumblings
Touched up.
Held down.
The common room sofa
sags under a tangle of boys on top of me:
'Ooh – you like that, don't you?'
Hot adolescent tears and
a final release.

Sixteen taunting voices follow me
as green-faced, I cycle home.

Father confronts the housemaster.
Next day, the housemaster confronts me:
'These things are dealt with in school, young man,
there was no harm done, after all.'
My fault. And, after all,
they play rugby for the school.

Twenty years pass
till I dare to come back.
Boys play cricket, laugh and run,
but I, alone,
wander to a deserted room.
The old, offensive sofa's gone.
It's clean, it's tidy,
cheery posters for all to see:
In here, they teach RE.

This poem expresses the beginning, and a sort of end, of the homosexual abuse I suffered as a teenager. Some Christian friends finally made it clear to me not only that it was not my fault, but also that I had a right to be angry about what had happened. The logic was this: I am an adopted son of God. Therefore Jesus is both my brother and my king. If Jesus is my king and my brother, what does that make me if not a prince? How dare they do that to one who is God's prince!

I don't know whether I'll ever be completely over the abuse: even today, I can get nervous if a man who is bigger than I stands close behind me! However, I no longer have nightmares, I can discuss what happened without dissolving into tears, I have learned something about my value to Jesus, and can see a certain heavy irony in the current use of the room where I was abused.

'It is for freedom that Christ has set us free' (Galatians 5.1). There are any number of reasons for the gap between that promise and its fulfilment. Intercession means 'standing in the gap'. As you meditate on Isaiah 61.1, you might bring individuals to mind before God, standing in the gap for them.

Monday

Jesus travelled about from one town and village to another, proclaiming the good news of the kingdom of God. The Twelve were with him, and also some women who had been cured of evil spirits and diseases: Mary (called Magdalene) from whom seven demons had come out; Joanna the wife of Chuza, the manager of Herod's household; Susanna; and many others. These women were helping to support them out of their own means.

(Luke 8.1–3)

We hear so much about those 12 first great apostles, the men who gave up everything to follow Jesus. We hear rather less about Joanna and Susanna, who also followed him and even supported him out of their own means. I can't remember a single sermon or book ever mentioning them. By contrast, Mary Magdalene has caught the imagination; and she does keep appearing of course, at the cross, at Jesus' burial. She is also the first to see him risen from the dead. Jesus, against the culture of his time, refused to see women as inferior to men. He talked with them, healed them, cared about them, let them follow him. A woman's testimony didn't even count in a court of law then, and yet Jesus chose this particular woman for perhaps the most important 'testimonial' role ever.

Mary Magdalene was known primarily as a woman oppressed by demons. Whatever that meant exactly, she must have been a damaged individual. Her 'demons' must have affected her behaviour, tormented her, isolated her from society. People would have dismissed her as mad, bad and dangerous to know. But Jesus set her free. No wonder she would have done anything, gone anywhere, for him.

* * *

I guess most of us, if we're honest, have some kind of 'mini-demon' that haunts us: a fear or memory perhaps, which surfaces when we're least expecting it and twists our behaviour, thoughts or relationships. It may simply rob us of sleep or drive us to more action than is good for us. For some people, this kind of oppression isn't trivial or transient but affects their whole lives. What Easter hope is there for them? A woman in her late forties told me her story:

> Yvonne was a disturbed young woman, angry and bitter. If anyone so much as touched her arm she would bite them. Unsurprising, perhaps, considering she'd spent her early years in a locked room from 8.00 am until 6.00 pm and then suffered sexual abuse every night. Later, being disabled, Yvonne lived

in various residential schools and institutions but abuse continued to make a nightmare of every holiday. At the age of 23, she refused to return home. Her key-worker spotted bruises and asked where they came from.

'I can't tell you, it's a secret,' Yvonne said. Eventually she did tell a Christian woman who had counselling experience and who had befriended her. Yvonne started to trust God herself – a little bit, anyway. Later this same friend took her to a theological college in Kent, where a Roman Catholic opera singer spoke honestly about his own life. 'I can be whoever I want on stage,' he said, 'put on a mask, act, play a part. But in life, if I'm honest, I feel awful. I suffer from depression.' Something in Yvonne identified deeply and she began to laugh. She couldn't stop. Before she went home someone prayed for her and she felt the pent-up anger of years drain away. Though she's had to deal with issues of anger since then, it's been easier and she's been able to open up more and more about what happened in that locked room of her childhood.

Previously Yvonne had felt isolated from other people. She had felt as though she didn't live in their world (the real world), that she couldn't take part in it, couldn't have friends, couldn't know herself, even. But over the years she allowed one or two Christians closer, to listen to her and to pray. 'Someone used the illustration of weed-roots, particularly bindweed. You can pull it up and then it comes back again – just like me. I would take a step forward into life and then grab my old ways of thinking back again.' But Yvonne and her friends didn't give up. Today she feels that terrible room is no more to her than any distant memory. It no longer has power over her. 'I'm thrilled because I can now hold the children when helping with the crèche at church. I couldn't do that until I was 30. I worried that parents held their children in inappropriate ways and couldn't stand it when a mother kissed her child. It was all perfectly natural, loving behaviour but it used to churn me up. Finally I feel that I'm free of all that stuff. Thank God – and I mean that!'

As you draw closer to Jesus during this Lenten season, is he setting you free from 'bindweed' roots – from things which have haunted you in secret for years?

Tuesday

> Blessed is he whose help is the God of Jacob,
> whose hope is in the LORD his God,
> the Maker of heaven and earth,
> the sea, and everything in them –
> the LORD, who remains faithful for ever.
> He upholds the cause of the oppressed
> and gives food to the hungry.
> The LORD sets prisoners free,
> the LORD gives sight to the blind,
> the LORD lifts up those who are bowed down,
> the LORD loves the righteous.
> The LORD watches over the alien
> and sustains the fatherless and the widow,
> but he frustrates the ways of the wicked.
>
> (Psalm 146.5–9)

Comforting words – but only if they're true. Does God really always uphold the cause of the faithful oppressed or give food to his people when they're hungry? What about Christians in famine areas of Africa, or believers under persecution in Indonesia? Worldwide, plenty remain imprisoned for their faith, plenty remain physically blind or bowed down. Clearly God is on the side of right. He encourages – no, commands – his people to intervene on behalf of anyone who is marginalized or oppressed and unable to stand up for themselves. If God 'fails' it's because he chooses to work through his people, but those of us in prosperous countries often fail to get on with the job of taking his provision to those who need it.

* * *

Not all oppression comes as a result of war, poverty or persecution, though. I found Amy, a teacher-friend, amazingly helpful when we were going through difficult times with one of our teenage offspring because I knew she and her family had survived far worse. God had held her and them. Her children grew up to become givers-to, rather than takers-from, their families and communities. Amy and her family gave me hope because they were some years older than my contemporaries at church, whose perfect offspring doing noble Christian things around the world sometimes made me want to scream. Not all of Amy's family would call themselves Christians by any means, though they are all delightfully creative and spiritual people – and, in my opinion, are leaning towards Easter. Here's the story of one of her sons.

> Amy and Len thought their son Ed was happy doing the law degree he'd chosen. The first they knew of anything wrong was a call from the university, saying that he hadn't turned up at lectures or seminars for a while. Neither his parents nor the university had any idea where he was, until he phoned home. Len rushed off to pick him up from the London rail terminal. It turned out that, having suffered a nervous breakdown, Ed had spent the missing time riding up and down the train line.
>
> In his 'frozen hysteria' Ed reverted to a child-like state and, back home, sat on a wall at his old primary school, waiting for his mum to collect him. He also attempted to hang himself. It seemed that his family could do little except be there, which proved very distressing to all. Though Ed's younger brother in particular showed a real strength way beyond his years, other teenage siblings had their own troubles and Len himself suffers from bouts of clinical depression. Amy says her children have always been most precious to her. Although she wasn't a Christian at the time of Ed's breakdown, she did believe in God and acknowledged him as the source of the help and strength she found to get them all through.

Eventually, mental-health professionals decided Ed needed some neutral territory in which to recover and compelled him to go into mental hospital. As Amy sat in the back of the car holding his hand on the way there, she could feel him fighting his 'devils'. The next day, though far from cured, he was more himself again. Having realized what an awful thing his illness was, he'd started to fight it.

He met many down-and-outs in mental hospital. Later, in a private nursing home, gifted people laughed with and at him and awakened his interest in classical music. Becoming fully well again took time, but eventually he studied English at a different university, loved it and got a good degree.

Time passed. Ed began a successful teaching career. Later he worked in a sixth-form college fraught with staff tensions and needed medical help for another nervous breakdown. They told him he was suffering from previously undiagnosed diabetes.

After a year of help, medication and no work, Ed found a prestigious job in the highly creative environment of a drama college. But when stress piled in again he had his third breakdown. Amy worried all the more because he was living away from home. 'But an angel turned up, in the shape of a girl half his age who became a tower of strength.' There had been a succession of girlfriends previously but this one is still with him. 'She's my favourite person,' Amy said of her, 'calm but never soft, just what he needs!'

When Ed recovered he found work as a senior lecturer in a teacher training college where he's excelled, especially on the pastoral side because his experiences and sensitivity make him very understanding. Ed decided he wanted to give something back. Remembering the down-and-outs in that first mental hospital, and the help that the creative arts have been to him, he runs workshops for a very special theatre company made up of homeless people. Many are either drug or alcohol addicts or mentally ill – and he gives so much to them.

Ed is still fragile and can become depressed at times. Although he's not suffered another complete breakdown, his diabetes becomes a serious threat if he fails to look after himself. Amy weeps over him sometimes and he remains always in her prayers. But he's learned to recognize his strengths and limitations and she's incredibly proud of him. 'It's been a painful journey, for him and for us, but it's in the darkest times that we get the most help,' she said, 'and yes, I'd say my own faith has been strengthened through suffering.'

Thank God that he's with us for the long haul.

Wednesday

A woman was there who had been subject to bleeding for twelve years, but no one could heal her. She came up behind him and touched the edge of his cloak, and immediately her bleeding stopped. 'Who touched me?' Jesus asked. When they all denied it, Peter said, 'Master, the people are crowding and pressing against you.' But Jesus said, 'Someone touched me; I know that power has gone out from me.' Then the woman, seeing that she could not go unnoticed, came trembling and fell at his feet. In the presence of all the people, she told why she had touched him and how she had been instantly healed. Then he said to her, 'Daughter, your faith has healed you. Go in peace.'

(Luke 8.43–8)

People get oppressed for all kinds of reasons. I've just been talking with a friend whose National Health Service work involves her in counselling teenagers. Recently, she told me, she's seen a number of girls who believe themselves to be vampires. They started by cutting themselves (not uncommon for teens) then licked up the blood, got a taste for it and now tell her they have 'gone off' other food.

'What's behind all that, then?' I asked her, appalled.

'It's cultural. Their lives are empty. They watch *Buffy the Vampire Slayer* and similar programmes and actually believe themselves to be vampires, who can't stand sunlight.'

Horrible, isn't it? There's something about blood which makes most of us squeamish. Drinking it in any quantity is bad for you physically, let alone psychologically or spiritually.

The Jews had huge taboos about blood. They believed that life was contained within it; blood had to be drained from animals before they were eaten and menstruating women were considered ritually unclean. If anyone touched such a woman, he or she also became 'unclean', so women had to keep out of everyone's way during their periods. They couldn't worship God, either with their families or in the synagogue or Temple.

The woman in Luke's story had been bleeding for 12 long years. Living more or less in isolation, she'd spent all her money on doctors who had not been able to help her. Where did she find the courage to push into the crowd surrounding Jesus, and to touch the tassel of his rabbi's shawl which hung between his shoulder blades?

Jesus didn't shy away from the woman who had the effrontery (or desperation) to break the taboo. Instead he called her 'Daughter'. Commending her for her faith, he blessed her with his peace as well as his healing. Neither would Jesus shy away from 'vampires' or any whose shame, emptiness or damage keeps them under oppression. Never shocked as he reaches beyond social, religious, psychological or cultural norms, he demolishes barriers and allows us to touch him wherever we are. Do we allow others who suffer oppression to touch us in the same way?

* * *

Margaret Burtenshaw, an English midwife, visited a special hospital and witnessed the miracle which happens when oppression is turned into freedom – not just once but over and over again. She writes:

Face to face with poverty and pain, trauma and tribulation, suffering and shame, I walked across the courtyard towards a group of women who waited with quiet dignity. They sat, sheltering from the fierce midday sun, on slatted benches, their sadness apparent only in their eyes. Wearing coarse cotton dresses and shawls, brown and dusty from long journeys, they had come from the remotest areas of the country and could speak only dialects unknown to the rest of the world. This was Ethiopia.

The stories of these women were hidden behind eyes dulled by heartache and loss. However, nothing could hide the silent trickle of urine, which ran down their legs, forming wet patches on the ground beneath their feet. Nothing could disguise the strong scent of ammonia which emanated from them. These women had suffered untold misery. For some it stemmed from the religious ritual of female circumcision, performed in early childhood. For others, early marriage and teenage pregnancies had meant straining to give birth through an underdeveloped pelvis. This resulted in days of labour, dead babies and damaged bladders. Whatever the cause, the condition had made social outcasts of nearly all of them.

Someone, somewhere had told them they could get help at the fistula hospital in Addis Ababa. This sanctuary of peace offers a haven of hope to the helpless and oppressed. Skilled surgeons meet these women's needs with a degree of kindness and care which makes their faith in God visible, tangible. All who serve in this place uphold the Christian ethos.

Most of the women find healing and restoration in this place of miracles. They are given a new dress before they return to their villages and start again. Some go on to give birth to live babies.

For a few whose trauma is irreparable, a home is found near the hospital in a special village where they can live out their lives in security and peace, with dignity and hope. Their mourning is turned to dancing and their sorrow to joy.

If you want to know more about the hospital, look at <http://
www.fistulafoundation.org/hospital> or read *The Hospital by
the River* by its co-founder, Dr Catherine Hamlin (Monarch,
2004). Meditate on these words, asking God what they mean for
you and for others: 'You turned my wailing into dancing; you
removed my sackcloth and clothed me with joy' (Psalm 30.11).

Thursday

The crowd joined in the attack against Paul and Silas, and the
magistrates ordered them to be stripped and beaten. After they
had been severely flogged, they were thrown into prison, and
the jailer was commanded to guard them carefully. Upon receiving such orders, he put them in the inner cell and fastened
their feet in the stocks. About midnight Paul and Silas were
praying and singing hymns to God, and the other prisoners
were listening to them. Suddenly there was such a violent
earthquake that the foundations of the prison were shaken. At
once all the prison doors flew open, and everybody's chains
came loose.   (Acts 16.22–6)

I know a man who says he has to watch his tongue whenever
he returns from visiting Christians in developing countries.

People in my English home church complain about feeling
oppressed because they have a headache, or because someone
said something that wasn't very nice to them last week. There's
no point my giving them an earful. That's what I feel like doing
though, having seen Christians in appalling situations who, instead of grumbling and feeling sorry for themselves, are praising
God, being generous and forgiving.

If I'd been 'severely flogged and thrown into prison', unjustly
at that, I don't think I'd sing hymns to God in the middle of
the night. Maybe I'd manage a few panic prayers. I'd also be
wallowing in fear and despair of my own making.

Not all Bible (or contemporary) stories of persecution end with the prison doors being flung open. Paul (we believe) and many of the other early church leaders died for their faith – yet weren't oppressed on the inside. One of the first, Stephen, prayed as they were stoning him, ' "Lord Jesus, receive my spirit." Then he fell on his knees and cried out, "Lord, do not hold this sin against them." When he had said this, he fell asleep' (Acts 7.59–60). These people were following Jesus who, mocked, stripped and beaten, endured a prolonged public death alongside common criminals. He resisted fighting back, resisted resisting his enemies and drank the cup God was asking him to drink. He prayed forgiveness on his torturers then quietly commended his spirit to God. And God vindicated him, setting him gloriously free on the first Easter morning.

* * *

I met Rachel Komara at a mutual friend's party. I knew how much my friend valued Rachel's leading of a small intercessory prayer group at their church. Rachel seemed well educated and radiated peace, but otherwise appeared ordinary enough. I asked where she came from and, when I found out, commented with lamentable understatement that Sierra Leone was a troubled place and assumed she'd escaped unscathed. Only later did I learn her story.

> I should have been terrified, in despair – so many armed men, throwing me in prison. I'd done nothing wrong, except be the wife of the Inspector General of Police. This was just after a military coup in Sierra Leone and they aimed to destroy anyone they thought might oppose them. I understood the distress my husband and children would be in at my arrest but my faith became stronger, not weaker, especially when another Christian in the prison started telling me how great God was. I found I

couldn't stop praising him – and remembered then how St Paul had done the same.

When my husband gave himself up to the military, they released me: they'd only wanted me as a kind of hostage. Meanwhile they'd vandalized our house and removed everything from it. Kind relatives had looked after our children and my disabled mother but our lives became harder and harder as I struggled to support them.

A big trial found my husband not guilty, but that didn't stop the military executing him illegally. I first heard about it as an item on the national news. And then my married daughter called from England where she worked as a nurse. She had been sending us some money but now her husband had suffered a brain haemorrhage and died, leaving her with two pre-school children. Would I come and help her?

In England I wasn't allowed to earn money but a local Methodist church welcomed me. I run a prayer group there, help with pastoral and hospital visiting and, having continued the biblical studies I'd started years before in Sierra Leone, passed my local preacher's exams. I began preaching on the circuit in late 2003. At the time of writing I'm still unsure if the Home Office will let me stay in Britain. The uncertainty makes life hard, but I do know how great is God's faithfulness.

Thank God that the faithfulness of the Rachels of this world bears witness to his faithfulness, and pray for all those who are being oppressed in such extreme ways, especially for refugees.

Friday

Then the governor's soldiers took Jesus into the Praetorium and gathered the whole company of soldiers round him. They stripped him and put a scarlet robe on him, and then wove a crown of thorns and set it on his head. They put a staff in his right hand and knelt in front of him and mocked him. 'Hail, king of the Jews!' they said. They spat on him, and took the staff and struck him on the head again and again. After they had mocked him, they took off the robe and put his own clothes on him. Then they led him away to crucify him.

(Matthew 27.27–31)

Oppression – what hope can that bring? How can a man in the position described above bring freedom to others – a man betrayed by his own people, his own friends, as well as the foreign invaders who oppress his whole country? Strange, isn't it? I wonder how much of our own freedom we owe to people, other than Jesus, who have endured oppression, paid for our freedom with their lives too?

* * *

A friend, Debra Elsdon, sent me a poem she wrote. It made me think more about Jesus' death – the power in it, as distinct from the power in his life on earth.

Hand signals
Wood roughened and sun-stained, hands work-soiled,
before, finger curled, he beckoned and they came.
When faith fled, he raised a palm, wind buffeted,
commanded calm and stilled a storm.
On a Sabbath day wheat ear finger-crumbled,
chaff flew, creed tumbled, truth was freed.
While frowns gathered, children felt the hand-heavy blessing
on their curls – professing, 'Such is the Kingdom of God.'
Finger-formed poultice swept blind lids,
revealed the light long hid, curse lifting.
The healer's hands grasped tables, shekel heavy,
overturned each one. Cleared a way – declared salvation's day.
Night huddled, garden bounded, Heaven commanded.
Obedient hands, cup-turned, received a bitter gall.
Fingers numb, tendons torn, body rope-lashed,
hands thorn-gashed against a splintered scaffold.

Is there healing for the healer's hands?

The marks of love for all to see,
he bears them through eternity.

On a lighter note, Debra also wrote (I hardly dare mention it
in the same breath, though I'm sure Jesus wouldn't mind)
about a certain raucous, hilarious, anarchic, wintertime the-
atrical production which only the apparently strait-laced English
are free (or mad?) enough to enjoy. The fact that those who
took part in this pantomime were 'under sentence' from cancer
says something to me about refusing to be oppressed, about
choosing joy and freedom.

The South East Cancer Centre Players were planning their 2003
pantomime, *The Sleeping Beauty*. My mother-in-law Joy, also
their director, asked me to write the script. The number of speaking roles kept being expanded due to demand – and to diminut-
ive, quiet Joy persuading the most unlikely people that what
they wanted most in the world to do was to dress up, sing solo
in public for the first time in their lives, and . . . er . . . fly.

Many of the actors were not in the best of health, some had
undergone surgery, many were receiving treatment which might
mean they wouldn't be fit to attend rehearsals. In spite of this
they learned lines and dance steps; they scheduled fittings for
costumes and built scenery; they patched themselves up in
whatever way they could to make rehearsals and deadlines.
Throughout, Joy would adjust, chivvy and encourage the con-
sistently shifting cast and crew. She's organized 12 shows there
in six years. Every time there comes a point when it looks certain to be a total disaster, beyond all rescue. That's when she
turns to God, 'I can't do any more: over to you!' The Centre
isn't a Christian organization but Joy's faith is strong and she's
learned to expect some miracle within the next 24 hours.

Someone who never dreamed she would appear on stage
stands up and sings a solo before all those people; someone

who's been given two months to live manages to perform eight months later, having kept going through sheer determination – that's hope, that's freedom, that's refusal to be oppressed by any diagnosis.

Performed in Croydon's 750-seat Fairfield Halls, the panto that year was a sell-out as usual, the enormous swell of good-will palpable from curtain-up. Friends and family cheered as the cast belted out a show tune, hooted with laughter at improvised wit, applauded as the lovingly crafted helicopter was lowered onstage to take the Princess and Prince away (don't ask!). When the Prince left the stage with the Brazilian dancers to mambo with the audience he twirled me around, saying: 'Do you recognize your script?' 'Scarcely a word,' I answered.

The Sleeping Beauty and the Lost City had finally included a chat show, an *Indiana Jones* sub-plot, a climactic battle involving the forces of good and evil, Spider-Man, Wonder Woman in full flight, and a lot of singing. My name appears on the programme, but the life, determination and sheer guts of people making plans against an uncertain future really authored the show.

Pray for those suffering from oppression, thinking especially of those enduring physical persecution or the oppression of illness and suffering.

Saturday

Betrayal at supper

So, he chose the dangerous path in coming to Jerusalem. I came to accept the wisdom of that. I reckon he saw it as a clever challenge. We know he has extraordinary powers. He raised at least two people from the dead to my certain knowledge, so there's no doubt that he could avoid his own death, even now! I understood his strategy – or thought I did. He'd come to power not through the rabble nor through us pathetically few disciples but through some-thing supernatural. I could just see him blasting away the Romans and his Jewish enemies, standing on the Temple Mount raising a storm, like a Moses or an Elijah, only ten times stronger, putting the fear of God into the lot of them, bringing his Kingdom in.

But this, this is madness. It's shocking. Everyone knows there are servants and there are slaves. There are the washed, the pure, and there are those who do the washing. It's the lowest slave who gets to wash the filth of our dusty roads off the stinking feet of travellers before they sit down to eat. Whoever heard of a rabbi, let alone a king or Messiah, doing that? Whoever heard of any kind of revolutionary leader holding himself in such low regard? Jesus promised us freedom from oppression – and about time too. God's chosen people have known oppression long enough. Now that Jesus has changed his tune, I for one have no intention of following him further into the bondage of slavery!

It's almost as though he's gone mad. Listen to what he's saying now. 'You also should wash one another's feet.' All those demons he cast out – they've turned on him. Someone needs to stop him, before he kills himself and us.

What's that he's whispering? 'One of you will betray me.' Too right, someone needs to do something, or this madness he's fallen into will betray us all.

(Imagined from John 13)

Lord, your Kingdom works by natural laws which often appear upside-down to us. Slaves are the most free, the lowest are highest, the weak are strong, those who suffer are blest, those who mourn are happy and the love of the meek who are betrayed and abased does triumph. Help us to see, not with Judas' eyes, but through the eyes of the writer of the Fourth Gospel the mystery of exactly how it was that you showed the disciples 'the full extent of your love' as you washed their feet.

God's love is made perfect in weakness,
Christ's weakness, your weakness,
not in my or your perfection.

Christ's love is made perfect in sorrow,
his breadth makes a narrow place
soar to wide horizons,
turns a fleeting second
into time for eternity.

Reach out to him in that second,
in that narrow place,
that sorrow or weakness,
and 'I AM' will hold you
with all that he is.

Despair to hope

Second Sunday in Lent

> To proclaim the year of the LORD's favour . . .
> to bestow . . . a garment of praise
> instead of a spirit of despair.
>
> (Isaiah 61.2, 3)

The phrase 'a spirit of despair' implies something which is not only deep but all-pervading, a switching-off to the chance of anything good ever happening again. Although human beings can certainly feel a spirit of despair, even when evil and destruction reach their peak, even at the cross, God pours his favour out.

Despair leaves no room for hope or anything else. Yet there may come a point (or, more realistically, many points) when someone may choose to begin taking off its stifling black garments, accepting in their place clothing which feels less comfortable, less appropriate, perhaps – the bright shawl of praise, the robe of hope, faith, even love. Isaiah's imagery prefigures Paul's:

> You have taken off your old self with its practices and have put on the new self, which is being renewed in knowledge in the image of its Creator . . . Therefore, as God's chosen people, holy and dearly loved, clothe yourselves with compassion, kindness, humility, gentleness and patience.   (Colossians 3.9–10, 12)

* * *

I talked to Jennifer Louis whose poem appears in the Introduction to this book. She has lived more than half her life in

Russia, having married Victor, a Russian translator, in 1958. They worked together in journalism and wrote travel books in English. When he died in 1992 Jennifer drew comfort from the Russian Orthodox way of mourning: special services and wakes on the third, ninth and fortieth days, then continuing 'birthdays' and 'death days', complete with cakes, candles and stories. She also drew comfort from the poetry which flowed from her during the four-and-a-half years following her husband's death, stopping only when her grieving was complete. Writing poems in simple language that her Russian friends could understand allowed her to explore not only the past and her current feelings, but all kinds of everyday experiences.

Jennifer showed me a poem which she wrote after the 'fortieth day' service. Some of the thin taper-candles from the cemetery had been only partially burned. She took them home and placed them alongside the laughing photograph of Victor which had been on display for the service. She had been thinking about how God lets go. 'Let there be light,' he said. 'Let my Son be born and live on earth.' 'Let the children come,' said Jesus, 'Let him have your cloak also,' 'Let your light shine before men.' And then God said the most astounding thing of all: 'Let my Son die on a cross.' God lets us go as well, even though it causes him pain. In the same way, Jennifer had to let Victor go; she wouldn't have wanted him to suffer with his illness any more. Seeing a pattern in this letting go, she wrote a poem about burning the remaining candles.

When a candle burns with brightest flame,
Flares up, sheds light, and I repeat your name,
Light spreads around and shadows disappear
And I've no doubt at all that you are near.

While the candle burns with steady glow,
Unflickering and silent, so I know

That I can rest, relax, draw strength for what's ahead
And talk to you awhile, remember what you said.

As each candle burns itself away,
Begins to sputter, fail and die right down,
So I grow drowsy, happy, dreamy,
Knowing we all, like candles, have our own short span.

Before it goes right out
There's but one last brave flare.
Then just a twisting, smoky spiral
And the smell of candle in the air.

Just as the candle's ending seemed right, so perhaps the
'garment' of despair needs to be 'let go' for washing. Jennifer
wrote another poem soon after Victor died, which acknowl-
edges the need for time to do its work in grieving, the need to
experience pain and also gentleness. But the poem is full of
quiet hope. Jennifer pictures women of the Russian countryside, rinsing their freshly washed clothes in the river; the writing
of the poem brought her some hope and healing of its own.

Time, that washes out all stain of pain
With endless rinsing,
Pouring out grey, cloudy scum,
Flooding in again, again, transparent, clear with each new day
To drive away yet another trace of sadness –
Be gentle as you wring my human heart
In your own ageless hands,
Squeezing out these few last drops
Which turn to words upon my page.

One icon of humanity grown beyond God relates to the legen-
dary but heroic Sisyphus, condemned to push a heavy stone
uphill for ever, because, on nearing the top, inevitably it would
roll back down again. Meditate on Easter in terms of letting
go, of letting someone else move the impossible stone.

Monday

'I, the LORD, have called you in righteousness;
I will take hold of your hand.
I will keep you and will make you
to be a covenant for the people
and a light for the Gentiles,
to open eyes that are blind,
to free captives from prison
and to release from the dungeon those who sit in darkness.'

(Isaiah 42.6–7)

These words are addressed to God's 'servant', an important figure in Isaiah. While he takes on several shapes, here he is a messianic figure – God's 'chosen one in whom I delight'. He is anointed with God's Spirit to bring 'justice to the nations' (*Messiah* in Hebrew, or *Christ* in Greek means 'anointed' or 'chosen one'.) Isaiah describes this servant-messianic figure as far gentler than the one whom the oppressed Jewish nation later hoped would deliver them from Roman occupation. 'He will not shout or cry out or raise his voice in the street. A bruised reed [pipe] he will not break and a smouldering wick he will not snuff out.' What extraordinary gentleness from God. Even if they still have a little light and music left in them, people who are bruised and almost without hope are all too easy to break or snuff out. God shows his strength, not through some violent overthrowing of evil power but through his persistence and goodness: 'In faithfulness he will bring forth justice; he will not falter or be discouraged till he establishes justice on earth.'

Faithfulness, justice, righteousness, patience, steadfastness, gentleness, hope – these are all fruits of the Spirit. In today's Bible passage we recognize not only the work that God intended Israel to do as she served as his 'light for the Gentiles' but also Jesus' own commission and purpose on earth. We recognize our own purpose too, for John 14.12 says, 'Anyone who has faith in me will do what I have been doing. He will do even greater things than these, because I am going to the Father.' Should we find ourselves in the position of being hope-bringers, of releasing someone who has sat in the darkness of a real or metaphorical dungeon for years, let's remember to be gentle, for even a little light can dazzle. More than some spectacular gift of opening prison doors, we'll need the fruits of the Spirit, which grow slowly and often in secret, right through the winter storms of our own lives. And we'll need to know in our very selves the truth of these verses, to have experienced God's Servant-Son bringing us hope when we had none.

* * *

Today's verses became very special to talented young artist Simon Lord, as he struggled with issues that were ruining his life.

> Working in a Christian bookshop, I observed that customers can be just as rude as they are anywhere else. But then I was looking for an excuse, on that blackest of mornings, to bite back and let everybody know how I was feeling. A woman stood in everyone's way as she read the same book for almost an hour. She approached me and would have got an earful, except that I heard her saying, 'It's so difficult to choose a book on depression. How do you know which one is going to help?' I found myself telling her that I too suffered from depression – something hard enough to share with the people closest to me, never mind a complete stranger. We spoke for about an hour. She detailed everything I had suffered since my early teenage years. It was as though she knew my very mind, it was like praying.
>
> Although I'd begun life with a wide-eyed love for the world, my teenage years were dominated by a depression that had gradually stagnated into my early thirties, making everything

seem futile, sabotaging my dreams of creativity, my relationships, my emotions. When I was sad I fell into despair; when I
was happy, I waited nervously for the inevitable fall.

When my mum died of cancer, the Christian friends who had
prayed for her healing continued to praise and believe in God.
That shocked me into wondering if there was more to life than
my own problems. Maybe God was real? I joined a church, left,
joined another, married my girlfriend . . . One night a guest
speaker at our church home group invited people forward for
prayer. I felt myself resisting, holding up a shield of fear. For
the first time in the three years I had been a Christian I was
absolutely suicidal and could feel nothing but despair. That
night I walked along the sea front, crying out to God.

It was the next morning that I talked with the woman in
the bookshop – and afterwards asked people at my home group
to pray for me. That proved emotional and painful, a live spiritual
battle. The following day, while writing, I felt a sharp pain in
my head. This happened twice, followed by a tangible peace and
reassurance that I had been fixed. God had repaired the wires
and connections that had been broken for years. I fluctuated
over succeeding months, particularly through winter, but within
weeks of that prayer, my emotions had become incapable of
falling to the once-familiar dark depths. I could be sad without
feeling suicidal, and happy without feeling anxious. God restored
the emotional capacity that he wanted me to experience, gradually making me whole again. I have worn the spiritual armour
described in Ephesians, Chapter 6 doggedly, sometimes clum-
sily, but God is teaching me to stand firm in him. Now I have a
passion to pray for others with a voice that once was stifled.
When I am tempted to feel negative, I walk in the confidence
that God is holding my hand and that he fully intends to keep me.

Pray for the light of God's hope to reach any you know who
find themselves trapped in some kind of a 'dungeon'. Ask that
he send his servant to them, but first count the cost should
that servant turn out to be you.

Tuesday

Why do you say, O Jacob,
and complain, O Israel,
'My way is hidden from the LORD;
my cause is disregarded by my God'?
Do you not know?
Have you not heard?
The LORD is the everlasting God,
the Creator of the ends of the earth.
He will not grow tired or weary,
and his understanding no one can fathom.
He gives strength to the weary
and increases the power of the weak.
Even youths grow tired and weary,
and young men stumble and fall;
but those who hope in the LORD
will renew their strength.
They will soar on wings like eagles;
they will run and not grow weary,
they will walk and not be faint.'
(Isaiah 40.27–31)

God is a God of new beginnings, of surprises. If his timing doesn't fit neatly with our own sense of urgency, with our impatience, it's not because he's fallen asleep or is disregarding us. He is the great I AM, eternally present in our action and our waiting, in our weariness, our suffering, our lost-ness. He knows where we are, and knows the path ahead, even if we can't see it, for he has the perspective of an eagle. In Isaiah 40.22, just before the opening of today's passage, the prophet states that God 'sits enthroned above the circle of the earth, and its people are like grasshoppers.' That could make him seem remote, uncaring, except that, 'He gives strength to the weary and increases the power of the weak.'

Just as he is eternally present in time, so he is present in all of space – from the tiniest part of an atom to the farthest galaxy – caring for all, sustaining all. No wonder that we prisoners of time and space cannot hope to fathom his understanding. But we can put our hope in him. And what a God to hope in! This picture of being bogged down, weary, defeated, faint . . . and then of soaring on eagle's wings is but a pale reflection of the spirit within the Easter story.

It's all too easy to dismiss both pictures as irrelevant to 'poor little old me, right now'. It's hearing about the little things, the little extra, generous details in the way God has restored hope to someone which encourage, literally en-courage, me to hope in him again.

* * *

I got to know Lorna McDougall in wild late October storms, tramping around Cornish cliffs and rock-pools. My family had rented a farm cottage for the half-term holiday. A friend, who had moved from our church to be part of a team reinvigorating a dying one in multi-cultural inner London, rented the adjacent cottage and brought Lorna along. Lorna had moved from her home in Scotland to train in evangelism at the fast-growing church for one year. She stayed for ten, teaching cello and piano in local schools and leading worship in the church. In her gentle way, she befriended and helped all kinds of people, giving, always giving so much.

It's always a delight to spend time with Lorna and we'd meet up with her and our mutual friend once or twice a year. Latterly, Lorna was feeling unsettled, worn down. She had some concerns about her church: her vision and its vision didn't seem to match as well as they had done. More importantly, she felt the need to return to her roots in Scotland, that God was calling her back there. She took a holiday in the Outer Hebrides, spending time on her ancestors' island.

'I connected so strongly with the land, drunk in the Holy Spirit in a way that I hadn't done before,' she told me. 'I found deep healing, peace and rest just spending time in the quiet, walking and driving around. As to when I'd return and to which part of Scotland, I wasn't sure.' She had left Scotland partly because her church on the mainland had become very controlling. Unwise, then, to return to the town where she'd grown up. Gradually over years in London she'd built up enough work to support herself as a single woman. If she moved to a part of Scotland where no one knew her, how would she find pupils quickly enough? So frustrating that her longings for the mountains, the space, the people of her homeland had been raised, with little realistic hope of their being fulfilled – what was God doing, we wondered?

And then we had a phone call. Lorna was moving to Scotland in a couple of weeks. A friend who had belonged to the same London church while training at a big teaching hospital was now working as a doctor in Inverness and renting a large farmhouse in nearby countryside. It had a spare bedroom and several downstairs rooms. Perhaps Lorna could teach music in one of them, instead of hurtling around London schools?

It still seemed risky but, sensing God was with her, Lorna put her hope in him and moved in July 2002. Almost immediately the manager of a local piano supply business assured her there was more demand than supply for piano lessons in the area and promptly lent her a piano. He was less optimistic about opportunities to teach the cello; but soon Lorna had a good supply of students for both instruments. Word whizzed round about the 'new cellist in town' and soon she was in an orchestra and a string quartet.

She also took an early opportunity to visit the local sailing club and the first people she met there were a Christian couple who loaned her a sailing dinghy (it happened to be her favourite class of boat) and became great friends. Lorna and Helen drew together a group of women who now meet for lunch on Fridays for friendship, prayer and to worship God. It's proving an oasis for many in a busy week.

In the handful of houses around the farmhouse several neighbours are Christians and three of them have started meeting on Mondays to pray for the area. Unusually for the Highlands, all are from different backgrounds – evangelical, charismatic and Roman Catholic. Their heartfelt unity centres in the love of Christ.

I find great hope in Lorna's story because I see God caring for her as a whole person: for her enjoyment of sailing and music, of sea, space and mountains; for her need for livelihood, friends and people with whom to pray and worship. And it's not something for Lorna alone. I see why she's there – she's acting as a catalyst, meeting all kinds of people, bringing them together in a way that wouldn't have happened without her. I see someone formerly on a blocked path who's been given soaring wings.

'May the God of hope fill you with all joy and peace as you trust in him, so that you may overflow with hope by the power of the Holy Spirit' (Romans 15.13).

Wednesday

Rejoice greatly, O Daughter of Zion!
Shout, Daughter of Jerusalem!
See, your king comes to you,
righteous and having salvation,
gentle and riding on a donkey,
on a colt, the foal of a donkey.
I will take away the chariots from Ephraim
and the war-horses from Jerusalem,

and the battle-bow will be broken.
He will proclaim peace to the nations.
His rule will extend from sea to sea
and from the River to the ends of the earth.
As for you, because of the blood of my covenant with you,
I will free your prisoners from the waterless pit.
Return to your fortress, O prisoners of hope;
even now I announce that I will restore twice as much to you.
(Zechariah 9.9–12)

'Prisoners of hope' – a striking phrase and accurate too: hope can be a painful thing. Without it we might do nothing except give up, hibernate, curl up and die on the inside. With hope we have to keep living . . . and risking. After leaving school, a friend took a succession of boring, but safe, office jobs until, on her first day in a new office, she found herself being addressed by a middle-aged fellow-typist wearing a salmon-pink hand-knitted cardigan. 'Do you know, we've just had the seventh rainy Sunday in a row?' Something snapped. My friend realized she could either continue talking about the weather all her life or risk handing in her notice. She bought a plane ticket to the other side of the world. Plenty of things went wrong . . . and, eventually, right. She remains grateful to the woman in the pink cardigan.

Risking disappointment, failure, even putting our life in danger, our human capacity for hope is extraordinary. Someone was telling me how, when the Tsar and his immediate family were shot during the Russian Revolution, more distant relations were pushed down a well and a bomb thrown after them. Some died immediately, others slowly. People who later recovered the bodies noticed how they had tried to help one another in that hopeless situation – ripping sumptuous gowns to bandage wounds, attempting to splint broken limbs. These horrific deaths were lent at least some dignity through expressions of hope and care.

What did Jesus feel, riding that colt into Jerusalem in fulfilment of this hope-filled prophecy from Zechariah? He knew it to be a dangerous place for him at that time; the enmity of the religious authorities was palpable. After his raising Lazarus from the dead caused a huge stir, now he was entering Roman-occupied Jerusalem, receiving honour, like a victorious king. I'd always thought that riding a colt, the foal of a donkey, was a sign of his humility, but found out that, in his culture, while a king rode out to battle on a war horse, he returned on a colt to signify victory and peace. Jesus knew part of his mission was to proclaim peace to the nations. That was his hope, but he hadn't even travelled outside of his own land – and he knew he would die very soon.

The hope that Jesus possessed journeyed along a painful, seemingly impossible, path; and yet he did 'free . . . prisoners from the waterless pit'. Looking at it from our time-perspective, he did cause his Kingdom to come in the lives of countless millions. He proclaimed God's peace to whatever nations would receive it. We, as characters in God's great story, are still prisoners of that same hope. We can still see it working out, or perhaps being held back for a while. Even in our brief, individual lives, hope comes and fades and comes again, even though at times it can feel as though we're holding on by the ends of our fingernails, screaming with the pain of it.

* * *

When Richard Narain, a young web designer, married Bev, who had three teenage sons from her previous marriage, they hoped for a baby of their own. Richard writes:

Hope came slowly, one step at a time, like walking a tightrope over a canyon.

Bev fell pregnant nearly a year after having her sterilization reversed. We were overjoyed. Nothing could have made us happier. I'll never forget the look on my stepson's face when we told him. I found it hard not to break into tears of joy when I told my family.

It never occurred to us that anything could go wrong and when it did the feelings were completely reversed. Joy became sorrow, elation turned to sadness.

The next time Bev was pregnant I didn't think the same thing would happen again. Even though an early scan showed potential problems, I felt we'd had our share of bad luck before and everything would be OK this time. We were again devastated when we lost the baby.

When we found out Bev was pregnant for the third time, there was none of the joy that we'd shared before. I've always thought it was a great shame that we couldn't enjoy that moment. We were pregnant – for now. We didn't know about tomorrow or next week or anything further than this moment. The future was a big question mark. Getting through each day was a titanic struggle.

At the time I thought I had faith. I believed it would turn out right this time. Now I realize it was not faith. Experience had shown the odds were against us, so there was nothing to have faith in. What we had then was blind hope, nothing more. Part of hope is to feel helpless and I did. There was nothing either of us could do to ensure nature took the path we wanted.

Two things got us through that tightrope walk: our relationship and time. The more time passed, the more hopeful we became. As days and weeks passed, our baby was growing and getting stronger. Milestones were reached. Early scans showed everything looked well. After a while Bev suspected she could feel movements and later I could feel them too. We heard a strong heartbeat at antenatal checks. One day we saw huge movements with our own eyes and we laughed and hugged. Gradually – very, very gradually – our fear changed through hope to happiness.

In those few early months all we had was hope. If there had been no hope, there would have been despair.

Lucy was born healthy and happy. She is a much treasured daughter, granddaughter and sister.

'Hope deferred makes the heart sick, but a longing fulfilled is a tree of life,' says Proverbs 13.12. God intended hope for dreams, not nightmares. Pray for those whose hope causes them pain.

Thursday

We continually remember before our God and Father your work produced by faith, your labour prompted by love, and your endurance inspired by hope in our Lord Jesus Christ.

(1 Thessalonians 1.3)

Paul told Corinthian Christians that the three things which remain eternally are faith, hope and love (1 Corinthians 13.13). Here he is saying that the Church in Thessalonica abounds in those three things – quite a commendation. This week we're looking particularly at hope. Why is it so important? If people live without hope they'll believe it's never worth doing anything – and that's despair. But Christians, apparently helpless in hopeless situations, still have hope in him. That 'hope which remains' has inspired countless Christians down the ages to take action. I tend to think of hope as something which gets things started – but here Paul links hope with endurance. Things often get worse before they get better. How we need the gift of hope to carry on when things go from bad to worse!

* * *

I met a couple while on holiday in Greece. They seemed ordinary enough at first – professionals, grandparents, fun to be with. But instead of arriving by charter flight like the rest of us, they had driven a van from Albania. Judy told me their extraordinary story.

No window glass unbroken, filth everywhere, desks and tables fit to be burned and a complete lack of hope in everyone she met – that's what faced head teacher Judy Smith when she went to Albania to help paint seven school classrooms in the summer of 1992. The country had only opened to outsiders a year before. Judy, who normally ran a primary school in Wales, had felt that she wanted to do something to help in Albania during her summer holidays. By that autumn she knew deep down that God was calling her to do something longer term in the land which had suffered for years under an atheistic dictatorship.

Judy and her husband, Mike, a mechanical engineer, were ordinary people, leading a comfortable life in Wales. What could they do? Within a year they had sold their home and left grown-up children, grandchildren and their respective careers (and pensions). Aged 57, they opened an orphanage in Elbasan, Albania. They called it 'The House of Hope'. The children they cared for were previously without hope. Some, who had been abandoned as orphans in hospital, couldn't even sit up. The backs of their heads had grown flat from lying down. It took between six and 18 months of loving help to teach them to sit, let alone walk. Others were offspring of young prostitutes, who would have sold them in Greece. Many of the children were difficult, disturbed and angry. It took all Mike and Judy's practical skills to care for them. At the same time they had to learn a new and difficult language and culture. It must have seemed an impossible task – and the situation was to worsen.

In the violent uprising of 1997, Mike and Judy refused the British Embassy's pleas to flee the danger, for 'who would look after the children?' Later they went with a rescue party and all 23 children to Tirana, staying there for six nights. On their return they counted 23 bullets in the garden. 'One for each child', Judy couldn't help but think. Yet The House of Hope not only survived but continues to do its job, caring for children who have no one. Mike and Judy themselves were at last able to hand the place over to others in 2002, returning to Wales for a well-earned retirement.

'We rejoice in the hope of the glory of God . . . [and] in our sufferings, because we know that suffering produces perseverance; perseverance, character; and character, hope. And hope does not disappoint us, because God has poured out his love into our hearts by the Holy Spirit, whom he has given us' (Romans 5.2–5).

Hold up before God's unstinting love those you know who face huge, ongoing challenges and feel their faith and hope are small and weak.

Friday

In this hope we were saved. But hope that is seen is no hope at all. Who hopes for what he already has? But if we hope for what we do not yet have, we wait for it patiently. In the same way, the Spirit helps us in our weakness. We do not know what we ought to pray, but the Spirit himself intercedes for us with groans that words cannot express. And he who searches our hearts knows the mind of the Spirit, because the Spirit intercedes for the saints in accordance with God's will. And we know that in all things God works for the good of those who love him, who have been called according to his purpose.

(Romans 8.24–8)

Waiting isn't fashionable. You're meant to know what you want (or ought to pray for) and go for it. Paul says we don't know, we can't see yet, that's the whole point. After all, the hope Paul is talking about here is a huge one, 'That the creation itself will be liberated from its bondage to decay and brought into the glorious freedom of the children of God' (verse 21).

Being weak appears undesirable: yet Paul says when we're weak we're strong, because that's when the Spirit helps us. When Jesus was on earth, most strong people wouldn't accept his help, while many who knew they were weak did. Paul's words bring hope because they are realistic. We certainly need help if big, cosmic hopes are in some way to work themselves out in our little lives. We dream in hope and, even when our dreams are God-given, we're often kept waiting. Paul seems confident that we wait 'patiently'. Not me. I often find myself groaning, and not necessarily in the Spirit. I'd prefer God to wave some magic wand of power than have his Holy Spirit groan in intercession. Yet he knows our hearts are complex, that change takes time. However big the stakes, he chooses to work with us rather than turn us into robotic slaves to his will. After all, that could never lead to 'the glorious freedom of the children of God'!

So, what are the hopes, dreams and long-term prayers that still cause you to groan? That God 'works for the good of those who love him and have been called according to his purpose' can sound horribly glib when hope is deferred, when we don't understand what is going on, and especially when bad things happen to good people. Blind optimism is foolish, but even when terrible things happen, looking back, we can often see a pattern where God has been rearranging the bad and the good.

* * *

Mary Huggins, an energetic 'people person', used to serve the community on her local Council. She writes:

> Electioneering always gave me a buzz, but this time it was different. I was fighting to keep the job I loved and the odds were

stacked against me. I was standing for the local Council – a Council on which I had served for four years. Boundary changes had put me in a different area with an unhelpful running mate. I felt very much alone. The day before the election I shared my worries with a friend. 'We must pray,' she said.

And so, there in the street, outside the village shop, we did. She had the right words. I was to trust and accept that what happened was God's will. I left feeling consoled and supported, but doubtful about trusting it all to God. After all, I knew what I wanted. I wasn't really prepared to accept what he wanted.

Election day passed in a flurry of activity. I went to the count with little hope. The result was announced – 35 more votes and I'd have made it. My friends were kind, the opposition was gracious, but all I could feel was failure and loss. At two in the morning I was driving home when I found myself saying out loud, 'OK, God. Perhaps you'll let me know now exactly what you do have in mind for me.'

I slept well that night. The following morning brought with it an amazing sense of peace and hope. My friend's prayer had been answered. And now, four years later I know that my prayer is answered – indeed is continually being answered. I have trained as a Crusader leader, learning much about young people and discovering that camping (even in the rain) can be fun! I have co-led an Alpha group, which has resulted in an ongoing house group. I have been authorized by the Diocese as a pastoral assistant and my role in the parish includes not only calling on those who need a visit but a special responsibility for small groups, which I see as a way to strengthen the life of the community of our church. What more exciting form of ministry can there be than seeing people grow in faith and confidence through the friendship and support which these groups give? I have even learned to make soup! This was for a weekly drop-in soup lunch which not only raised valuable funds over a two-year period but served as a friendly meeting place. The gifts I used and the skills I learned on the Council have been expanded in these activities and I have no doubt whatsoever that God has further doors that he will open to me.

Lord, your will is not always our will, but you know our hearts. You know what each of us really wants and needs far better than we do ourselves. Help our hearts to beat in time with yours. Help us to love what you love, to hope for the same things as you do, to intercede alongside your Holy Spirit. Help us to be patient as we wait for your pattern, for our little part of your world to be restored and to grow, for Easter to invade our space once again. Help us to justify your astounding hope in us!

Saturday

Thaddaeus, a disciple

Jesus used to pray, you know, a lot. 'Talking to his Father', he called it. He spoke out loud usually. Sometimes we could hear, but often he'd to go off somewhere quiet by himself, all night sometimes. I think the most amazing prayer we heard was one most of us didn't take in at the time – not properly. Please understand, Jesus had already been talking to us for ever. He knew what was going to happen and I think he wanted to spend those last few hours with us, to prepare us, to say goodbye and give us all he could. Talk about a tense time! This was just before we crossed the Kidron Valley to that olive grove – the one where we used to gather and eat some bread in the open air and listen to him and just be together. To think that Judas led his enemies to our quiet, special place . . .

The prayer Jesus prayed that night was written down years later. I didn't take much of it in at the time. Too confused and worried, even I had picked up that something appeared to be going very wrong. Jesus knew very well what he was facing, though.

Despair to hope

The Son of God about to be dragged before Jewish and Roman courts, mocked, flogged and crucified like a criminal and what did he talk to his Father about? Anguish? Despair? No. Glory! That the Father would glorify him through all this. Amazing. About to die himself, he talked about giving people eternal life.

Then he explained how we, his disciples, belonged to his Father. We were about to crumble, he knew that! But he told his Father, 'Glory has come to me through them.' 'Will come' I could have understood – we did all go on to do amazing things in the power of his Spirit. But what had we been like following our leader on earth? Misunder-standing him constantly, quarrelling among ourselves! We wouldn't have brought even the average rabbi any credit at all.

Then Jesus prayed about joy – not the word I'd use when facing crucifixion. He prayed that we would be one. Some hope, eh? Anyone else would have given up on us months, or years before. Even since his resurrection we haven't always been united. Holding a growing church together isn't easy. But things could have been far worse. It's good to know that he prayed – still prays – for our unity.

His final words were these: 'I have made you' (the Father) 'known to them, and will continue to make you known in order that the love you have for me may be in them and that I myself may be in them.' What hope, what faith, what love! Can you understand how amazing he was – and is? Can you understand now why to hope in him does not make me crazy?

(Imagined from John 17—18.3)

Cornered in a dark place, will you choose despair or hope? Spend some time reading through Jesus' prayer meditatively – and then perhaps talk over with him some of the questions which may be raised by the poem below. I wrote it in response to a photograph in the magazine of a Christian relief and development organization. It showed children learning their sums in an African refugee camp.

Take away?
They're taking away in a refugee camp.
It looks like a bomb site or rubbish tip.
While parents scavenge,
a teacher, in a scavenged jacket
stands by his scavenged chalk board,
picks a raised arm, thin, brown,
belonging to a boy who'll
eager-answer the next
take-away sum (borrowing required).
So why is this more hopeful
than all our adding up?

Darkness to light

Third Sunday in Lent

To proclaim freedom for the captives
and release for the prisoners.
(Isaiah 61.1)

Jesus not only quoted these words in his manifesto (Luke 4.18), he declared in the parable of the sheep and the goats (Matthew 25): 'Come, you who are blessed by my Father; take your inheritance, the kingdom prepared for you since the creation of the world. For . . . I was in prison and you came to visit me.' What an extraordinary, revolutionary thing to say. His society believed God blessed the rich and respectable, the well-washed, who visited the Temple regularly. God, in the darkness and disgrace of prison – unthinkable! Of course, prisons exist in the mind or soul and God is everywhere in a transcendental, other-worldly way. But Jesus goes on to say: 'Whatever you did for one of the least of these brothers of mine, you did for me.' He's identifying with actual as well as metaphorical prisoners, asking us to bring them hope too.

In Isaiah's and Jesus' time prisoners of war, or conscience, were thrown together in terrible conditions with thieves and murderers. Today at least some idea of corrective, restorative, redemptive justice has filtered into the justice systems of various Western civilizations, largely by the influence of Jesus' attitude. But prisons are still dark places. I've only been inside once, to visit a chaplain who was doing remarkable work, introducing tough guys on remand to new hope in Jesus. On the way to his cosy office I heard the endless clang of metal doors echoing down bare corridors, the constant locking and unlocking of double-barred doors. I felt the utter lack of colour, softness and silence, smelt the fear of one prisoner for another. A week, let alone a year, in that place could have driven me to darkness and despair. And yet this is a place where 'resurrections' can happen. People like that chaplain, David Powe, in his way, or my friend Judy in hers, are bringing light in the darkness, hope into hopeless situations.

* * *

Mother-of-three Judy Yates had an enviable life co-directing a travel company with her husband, but her story doesn't end happily ever after. Their eldest son died, aged 24, from a drug overdose, shortly after his release from yet another prison. That hasn't stopped Judy, with her amazing sense of reality, and of humour, in fighting to gain something better for others. Here she tells an earlier part of the story:

> It never occurred to me as he was growing up that my son would land up in prison. I had little interest in that world, knew nothing about it.
>
> My son developed a serious drug problem in his teens. We struggled to help him but, after a few nightmare years, he was sent down – for the crimes he committed to fund his habit.
>
> I went to visit him in a young offenders' institution, feeling deep shame and regret but not a little relief that at least I knew where he was, he had a roof over his head, three meals a day, and hey, maybe the prison could help him where we, his family, had failed.
>
> I stood with all the other prisoners' families and friends, in a queue outside the prison. We waited in freezing winter rain, the young and old, the fit and the infirm, as each visitor's paperwork was processed. Finally, when I entered the prison visits

hall and saw my son, I noticed he'd put on weight and had colour in his cheeks. I was pleased to see him looking so well, until he moved his arms. When his sleeve rolled up I saw raw wounds. Nobody told me he had been attacked. I was horror struck. He explained that he had done it himself. I'd never heard of self-harm. Why hadn't somebody warned me? What were they doing about it? I left that prison in tears.

As a member of a young offender's family I presumed that there would be someone in prison taking care of him, like a nurse in a hospital. Someone to watch over the boys, to show them the error of their ways and guide them towards law-abiding lives. I'd refused to send my son money and told him he should get a job in the prison. I didn't realize that there were no jobs to be had. That these boys, many of whom were il-literate, were locked up alone for 23 hours a day, seven days a week. No wonder they self-harmed.

Not long after that my son rang me. He was very upset be-cause the boy in the next cell had hanged himself. He said that one of the officers was in tears. I was so relieved to hear about the tears. That was the first indication I had that anyone cared about those boys.

I watched the news on television that night. Nothing. I scoured the papers. Nothing. A desperate teenager committing suicide in prison was not news.

I was appalled. Was this how modern-day Britain cared for their erring youth? Locking up teenagers in solitary confine-ment for 23 hours a day, in such distress that they would self-harm and commit suicide? I had no idea this was happening. I had to do something.

Soon afterwards I read about a prison monitoring organiza-tion, a collection of lay observers active in every prison in the country. I applied, and was accepted to join the board in the prison where my son had been held.

Having a son in prison opened my eyes to suffering and showed me how I could help. Since then, I have been privileged to watch as the prison service has installed systems aimed at helping young offenders. They are no longer locked up all day, but offered opportunities to improve their education, and literacy, get help with addiction problems, and gain skills to help their employment prospects on release.

It's not a perfect system, but it's a vast improvement on what it was, and I have gained pleasure in watching it change.

Can you pray for people in prison, staff and prisoners? Can you get involved in one, or in other dark places where people aren't free?

Monday

In the beginning God created the heavens and the earth. Now the earth was formless and empty, darkness was over the surface of the deep, and the Spirit of God was hovering over the waters. And God said, 'Let there be light,' and there was light. God saw that the light was good, and he separated the light from the darkness. God called the light 'day', and the darkness he called 'night'. And there was evening, and there was morning – the first day.   (Genesis 1.1–5)

Whatever the exact mechanisms of creation, deep truth lies within the story that, as God speaks, light emerges from darkness, order from chaos. These first words of the Bible reverberate with hope. I've always felt it must be pretty hopeless (as well as difficult) to believe that a freak accident made everything from nothing. For Christians on the other hand, there's great hope in knowing that God created us and the world – and loves his creation.

During Lent in England, light gathers as the days grow visibly longer. Although the sun is never very high in the sky, on bright days the air remains crisp, the shadows long. Only after Whitsun does the mellow flowering of high summer come. One balmy May evening, I sat staring up through a clematis-covered pergola at the full moon. Sometimes clouds veiled it, sometimes they blotted it out completely; yet the moon was always there, just as it always is, in our dark and in our day, remaining a globe in the heavens, whether we see it as full or the merest sliver, whether we have the best telescope in the world or are blind. Rivers flow, plants grow, the moon and sun rise whether or not we're there to see them. And after the night, day comes; after the winter, spring. When we're stuck in agonizing blackness, or experiencing the unending grey of quiet desperation, if we lose sight of God's constancy, sometimes creation's light touch reminds us that beauty still exists and helps restore our hope.

Some find the creative process itself a hope-bringing and loving activity, though far from easy. My daughter Hannah drew plans for a desk-tidy to make in her craft, design and technology lessons. She ordered some pine because it is soft and easy to carve, but her teacher, liking her work, produced with a flourish a large lump of hardwood. Hannah screeched – it was dirty and covered with spiders' webs. Her teacher explained that he had stored this piece of mahogany in his garage for 20 years, but felt her design would make good use of it. Grumbling that pine would have been easier, Hannah set about cleaning, then planing the oblong block to a roundish shape which would fit the lathe. The planing took three hours' hard labour. Turning on the lathe proved comparatively easy, then sanding consumed yet more hours and made her arms ache. But she produced splendid semi-circular book-ends which doubled as desk-tidies and was especially proud of them be-cause of all the work she had put in.

* * *

Today's Bible passage reminds me of God's lively creativity. So often amid the little things of life he creates order out of chaos, light in the darkness or something out of nothing – and surprises us.

Marina is employed in a day centre for people with profound learning and other disabilities. She and her colleagues work as a team with groups. Using whatever means they can to communicate, they offer dignity, choices and love. A creative person, Marina finds art or music reach some individuals when words won't. She loves the work but it's never easy. When she no longer knows what to do, Marina finds herself praying.

She leads the most demanding session of the week – music and movement with the most learning-impaired group. They are given access to different musical instruments and the team always has to work especially hard to bring any kind of order out of the hubbub. On this occasion nothing was going right. Then Marina heard her own voice saying out loud, 'God, help me!' Wondering what on earth a colleague standing nearby must think, she continued playing the piano. One man who was almost deaf started rapping out a particular rhythm on a xylophone. He'd never done anything like this before. Amazed, Marina matched her piano-playing to his rhythm. It caught people's attention. Suddenly they were all 'in the session' together. It was going so well that Marina realized she wasn't alone. God really was helping her. 'My heart was softened, my faith strengthened and I found new energy to continue,' she said.

On another occasion Marina wrote this poem about walking in woodland at night.

In the night silence comes, instead of light,
to fill the space with tranquillity.
What a different language nature speaks now.

Our usual routes felt asleep with the lack of light.
Where are we?

Common logic is unable to give us the answer.
We are trapped in the possibility
of being ourselves.

Stars feed us with the perfection of eternity –
another dimension, opening new routes . . .

Lord, you find so many creative ways to lighten our darkness. Show us how to work creatively alongside you, lightening the darkness of others, bringing harmony from chaos.

Tuesday

Why are you downcast, O my soul?
Why so disturbed within me?
Put your hope in God,
for I will yet praise him,
my Saviour and my God.
My soul is downcast within me;
therefore I will remember you
from the land of the Jordan,
the heights of Hermon – from Mount Mizar.
Deep calls to deep
in the roar of your waterfalls;
all your waves and breakers
have swept over me.
By day the LORD directs his love,
at night his song is with me –
a prayer to the God of my life.

(Psalm 42.5–8)

I do love this Psalm. Psychologists (and writers) know that each of us has our dark side, our shadow-self. Sometimes, in our efforts to be good, this side is driven deep into our subconscious. It seems we can't get at it, to bring it into the light.

Hurts, fears, jealousies and pains, though hidden and buried deep, sometimes affect our behaviour. Base impulses occasionally explode to the surface like geysers, spurting anyone standing in the way with the boiling, sulphurous spray of rage, lust or greed. Or our darkness finds its way to the surface in the slow ooze of sullen bitterness, resentment or depression.

We don't know why the Psalmist's soul is 'downcast'. We do sense his pain in remembering the times when he led his nation's festivals in the high praises of God. He tells us by contrast that he's now in agony, feeling battered and half-drowned, taunted by his enemies. Yet deep is still calling to deep.

God's depths are not shallow, inaccessible or silent. They call to the dark depths within each one of us. Despite his distress, even in the long night the Psalmist found God's song was with him.

Some people's temperament is very even. Others experience highs and lows – as I do, hating the deep, dark, painful places. But when God's song reaches me even there, then I know, in a way that can't ever be un-known, that his love is real and that his redemption can reach every part of me. Sometimes we can actually start the song ourselves. That requires a huge sacrifice of praise, because it's the last thing we feel like doing. Suddenly, as our song meets God's, his light shines even in the darkest night.

I found myself writing this in my journal the other day:

> If there are great holes and gaping tears in my life, you are the God of the gaps. The oil of your Holy Spirit can seep, then flow through my broken places, where my very fabric is weak, filling me until, out of my emptiness, others receive your drenching. Awaken my passion, for neither reason nor effort can bridge the gaps – but your presence, even longing for your presence, changes everything.

* * *

Morag Bramwell is a part-time legal secretary and mother of three from the Highlands of Scotland. She wrote down for me a recurring dream of a river which washes her as she sleeps.

> I dream of a river. It runs through my dreams, sometimes hidden away while my jumbled, upturned, sinful thoughts return to their pagan earthly places. My river-dreaming returns unexpectedly, tranquil amid the seeming chaos.
>
> I dream of a river. The river, the creator of the valley, gentle, century-long, slow and patient wearer-down of ragged edges, patient landscape-sculptor yielding to, yet moulding, the shape of the very mountains.
>
> The river? How can I begin to describe its effect upon me, dreaming, lying unremembered, winding its patient way through my other sleep-life? Just sometimes, the river rises, imprinting mysterious blue on my waking consciousness, a quiet reminder of that other life which awaits. Oh, but when I'm there . . . the welcome first walk into its clear blue-green water – the child in me bursts through. Sheer joy is in that cleansing plunge!
>
> Find me again, oh river, never wind away from my mountainside. Bring your clean waters to me and baptize me nightly, wash the pagan wildness, the earthly grime, the untamed dreaming fantasy which is my powerless will, and shape me into a rounded, grace-full thing.

Whether your spirit is singing or groaning today, relax just as you are and soak in God's river.

Wednesday

'I have come into the world as a light, so that no one who believes in me should stay in darkness.'   (John 12.46)

Jesus had to battle with darkness – the darkness of temptation, of Gethsemane, of the cross. He had to do battle with evil, ignorance and sheer pig-headedness in others. I guess the rest of us not only encounter but are a mixture of darkness and light. Coming from darkness into the light sounds wonderful at first, but sudden bright lights hurt the eyes. Perhaps we fear being burned up, like a moth drawn into a flame. Staying in darkness can feel far more comfortable for all kinds of reasons, not least because we wrongly perceive God's light and holiness as something frightening and, for us, unobtainable. The dynamic of Easter takes us beyond our struggles to obey complicated laws, beyond trying to reach God in our own strength, and empowers us to live according to his heart, his ways. It takes us out of 'you can't and you should' into 'you can and you will'.

It doesn't all happen at once. I've observed that God rarely shines his light on us at full dazzle, perhaps because he knows that we can't stand it. We let his light first into one room of our 'house' perhaps. It reveals that the room needs a good clean-out and so we're ashamed at first; but soon we're pleased not to be tripping over all sorts of rubbish which we hadn't seen in the darkness, and we're pleased to discover all kinds of good things too. Then, as we cautiously let a little bit of light into the next room, our hearts sink again.

Hope for something better comes at the cost of shame for what is there. But shame keeps us in the dark, so we need to let it go. Accepting God's light and hope means risking trusting him with the hidden, messy, dark parts of our lives. It can mean pain. Think of the terrible noontime darkness preceding the blazing light of the resurrection. When the Temple curtain tore in two it seemed like the end of everything. But that darkness, that tearing, let hosts of people previously excluded right into the light of the innermost presence of God.

* * *

I met Susan Holt on a couple of writing courses. Health problems, loss and a strangely serious upbringing had left her isolated and lacking in confidence in many areas of her life. She said, 'God loves me . . . so what?' Then, very slowly, she started discovering both him and her real self in a new way. A few years after I first met her she sent me a poem that she had written. I'm quoting it here with her permission – even though the imagery is not about light but about stirring a cake – and it's a Christmas, rather than an Easter cake, too!

Stirring
The deep stirring of a Christmas cake.
The currants have always been there
stuck in a clump,
the raisins also,
and even, hiding away, a sticky mass of cherries –
waiting for the Three Wooden Spoons:
Common Sense,
Thought,
God,
to come along.

To stir
through memory, talking, grieving
acknowledging hurt, anger
feeling always left outside.
To stir
through events, frustration, unhappiness.
To stir
deeply, yet gently.
To stir
through knowing and growing
and finally, at last, in the end, amazingly, flowing.

It feels physically deep this stirring.
Things are moving inside,
really changing.

The stirring continues.
The cake, the mixture, me,
starts to blend, to merge
finding space for the cream, the brandy of life.

The whole starts to make sense
and human emotions arise
from the solid, serious clumps.

Space is left:
space for living, loving, laughing,
space for enrichment, creativity,
space for getting close,
space for moving on –
forward, with interest, enthusiasm and belief.
And all because of a stir,
a big deep stir
at the bottom of my life's mixing bowl.

And who can say what the taste of the cake will be?
And who knows what the result of the eating will be?

What dark things show up when you walk closer to the light of Jesus' love? What does his light show up to be bright and exciting?

Thursday

It was now about the sixth hour, and darkness came over the whole land until the ninth hour, for the sun stopped shining. And the curtain of the temple was torn in two. Jesus called out with a loud voice, 'Father, into your hands I commit my spirit.' When he had said this, he breathed his last.

The centurion, seeing what had happened, praised God and said, 'Surely this was a righteous man.' When all the people who had gathered to witness this sight saw what took place, they beat their breasts and went away. But all those who knew him, including the women who had followed him from Galilee, stood at a distance, watching these things.   (Luke 23.44–9)

It's hard for us, knowing the end of the Easter story, to imagine what it must have been like for those who knew Jesus and 'stood at a distance'. They had followed him from Galilee. He was their life, their hope. The strange physical darkness of the sun ceasing to shine must have chimed with their own feelings that the world, or everything good in it, was at an end. And yet, in the darkness, the hardened Roman soldier in charge of the crucifixions that day saw something which perhaps he wouldn't have seen in the light: that this was a righteous man. Such an odd thing for him to say. Praising God – what an odd thing for him to do!

Then there was the tearing in two of the Temple curtain, which seemed at first a desecration of the holiest place. It turned out to be a token of the bursting out of God's holy love towards everyone, including the Romans, as he forgave the evil done to his own Son, opened a way into his presence and prepared to vindicate Jesus' righteousness by raising him from the dead. A few verses later, in Luke 24.4, women, still numb and cold with the darkness of death, encounter angels of light inside Jesus' empty tomb. Few of us have experienced anything like this dazzling transformation from horror and despair. Yet for those who have experienced the death of someone who was everything to them, with no resurrection, glimmers of light do come.

* * *

Retired botanist Margaret Dean writes about the time when her husband, having recently retired as a cancer specialist, was himself diagnosed with cancer.

Hope comes and goes like tides of the ocean, like waves on the beach. Sometimes only a tiny point of light or a faint glow behind the clouds.

My friend's husband was dying. 'A long dark tunnel with no light at the end,' she said, and he got worse.

My husband was ill too, in the next hospital bed. He was busy drawing out plans for a new water garden he imagined building. He improved, he came out of hospital, he sowed lots of seeds in the greenhouse, he dug out new flower beds, he edited a book, he booked a holiday. Then he got worse. There was no light at the end of the tunnel, but it was illuminated in bright colours all the way along. The hopeful tunnel was itself valuable and since he left, the light has continued to brighten lives. So foster the candle, open the curtains, blow away the clouds.

When going through a dark time, it can be helpful to write down the glimmers of light that you do see. I wrote this poem early in March one year after the repercussions of a tooth abscess led me to pain-filled weeks of feeling useless. To cheer us all up my husband took the children and me for a drive in the country and this is what I wrote back at home. You might find it helpful to meditate on how, during the often sad, dark days of Lent, signs of spring, of new life, are all around.

Dark! The woods are dark brown and dark
green only with tired pine, dusty holly, choking ivy.
'But look!' says a voice beyond the misty afternoon.
First willow's silver softness, then dangling, trembling gold –
catkins shine by the roadside
against the dark wood. Brown, I said? No, dark
purple with buds pent.
Revival signs! Next month nothing will stop
unimaginable volumes of fresh green
bursting from their holding darkness
to crown the lively wood.

Friday

For Christ's love compels us, because we are convinced that one died for all . . . that those who live should no longer live for themselves but for him who died for them and was raised again. So from now on we regard no one from a worldly point of view . . . If anyone is in Christ, he is a new creation; the old has gone, the new has come! All this is from God, who reconciled us to himself through Christ and gave us the ministry of reconciliation: that God was reconciling the world to himself in Christ, not counting men's sins against them . . . We are therefore Christ's ambassadors, as though God were making his appeal through us. (2 Corinthians 5.14–20)

Peacemakers and those who practise forgiveness offer hope to the world, or to those whose lives they touch, anyway. God's transforming us from darkness to light, from death to life, isn't simply nice for us: it's meant to spread. If people truly acknowledge him as King they'd treat each other according to his ways, not their own. But how? I've just watched a reasonably 'straight' two-hour presentation on television about the 'Moral Majority' in the USA. It showed large numbers of 'born again' and in many cases individually transformed Christians, effectively mobilized on the right wing of politics. They condemned homosexuality and abortions and fought for prayer to be allowed in state-run schools. It seemed to me that, in homing in so strongly on these issues, they had forgotten about great swathes of God's heart and ways, as expressed in the Bible. They didn't appear to share God's passion for the poor, were eager to stir up wars and appeared more concerned to condemn than to forgive. That's easy for me to say. Politics has never been my 'thing' and power tends to corrupt even that which may have started off good. I questioned whether it was possible to work with God, as his ambassador bringing light to a world darkened by evil, selfishness or simply indifference. Well, Christians do, be they 'ordinary' or exceptional . . .

* * *

The Revd Steve Elmes tells the story of a remarkable lady in his former church.

When Prudentienne arrived in England, recently widowed and with an eight-month-old child, she was full of grief and anger. In Rwanda she had witnessed members of her family butchered; then in Angola, her husband, a Brit, had been murdered. Prudentienne wanted to find a gun and take revenge. Yet her experience of being loved by her husband's family (Chris had worked for Oxfam in Rwanda where he met his African wife) and by members of the churches in Edenbridge brought about a miracle in Prudentienne. She chose to forgive. More than that, she decided to dedicate her life to working for peace and reconciliation in the Great Lakes Region of Africa.

One day Prudentienne came to share with me her vision for a Peace Conference in Edenbridge. She wanted to invite Rwandans, both Hutus and Tutsis, presently in exile around Europe, as well as delegates from other parts of the Great Lakes Region. It all seemed a bit unlikely. Yet Prudentienne was determined. Her plan was simply to get people eating, dancing and talking together – to begin to break through the hostility and find common ground. It came off, with some 50 African delegates descending on Edenbridge. It stretched us all – homes were opened, beds and meals prepared, many long debates were had and not a little frustration over time-keeping – and we all grew through the experience. Prudentienne was like a catalyst to the church and community in Edenbridge, teaching us about the hospitality of the Kingdom of God, pushing us over our normal boundaries. The conference was a great success, culminating in a declaration, agreed by all present, that was sent to the Rwandan and British Governments.

Darkness to light

Prudentienne continues to work for peace and still lives in Edenbridge with her son Mahoro, aged nine. Mahoro means 'Peace'. If ever a name was prophetic!

Forgiveness lightens darkness. If Prudentienne can forgive and make peace, who can you forgive?

> Ugly news from the TV shouts,
> 'Neglect! Hate! Spite!'
> But, Lord, your face is beautiful.
> Deep sorrow's in your eyes,
> and endless love as,
> against all odds,
> you hope in us.

Saturday

Mary at the cross

Did he bring me light or darkness? Light, I thought at first – enough light to trust, despite my fear, my feelings of utter inadequacy. Angel-light piercing the darkness. My cousin's husband, old Zechariah, freed from his dumbness to sing those bright words, 'The rising sun will come to us from heaven to shine on those living in darkness and in the shadow of death, to guide our feet into the path of peace.' Ancient Simeon in the Temple, recognizing God's salvation in my baby, 'A light for revelation to the Gentiles and for glory to your people Israel.'

My hidden dread, though, darkened like spilt blood when Simeon turned aside to me, whispering, 'This child is destined to cause the falling and rising of many in Israel, and to be a sign that will be spoken against, so that the thoughts of many hearts will be revealed. And a sword will pierce your own soul too.' I used to wonder, what did all this mean? How I would be able to bear such things? Yet in those early days our family experienced

*not only words but practical experience of the Light saving us
from death and darkness. I might have been stoned to death for
conceiving a child out of wedlock, had it not been for Joseph's
enlightening dream and his loving, wise response to it. And then,
the baby born, Herod's dark anger rising, another dream, a fleeing
in the night to a place where our people had known dark
oppression . . . In the first years of Jesus' life we walked through
dangerous darkness, but we were carrying the Light.*

*I spoke to few people as he grew; to whom could I speak? I
know what I saw and felt. Deep inside me a pool brimmed with
wonder. But as time went by my questions increased. How do
you care for Light which arrives in your house in human form
and needs mothering? No one had that responsibility before, no
one. And dear, faithful Joseph died long before I had to let Jesus
go, as all parents must let grown sons go. I could only watch and
pray as my extraordinary son started shooting his fierce lightning
bolts of love against the darkening clouds.*

*The storm seemed to break from every quarter at once, engulfing
Jesus and all who had been close to him. How could I bear watching my son die like that, you ask? Too many mothers had to in
those days. Public torturing-to-death had become common place
at the hands of our Roman oppressors. But how could God, who
had made all those promises, let this happen to Jesus?*

*Then, I thought, maybe I'd betrayed my son, not played my
role properly, not looked after him well enough. I couldn't leave
that horrific execution place though, nor could a couple of other
'weak women' who had cared about him – Mary from Magdala
and Mary my half-sister, who married Clopas. You know what
the word 'Mary' means? 'Bitter'. In the old story, that's what
Naomi asked to be called after her husband and two sons died.
Yet Ruth, my foreign ancestor, stuck by her. Yes, strange, isn't
it? We're named for Miriam, great Moses' sister; the name hints
at obstinacy and rebellion as well as bitterness.*

Darkness to light

Was that what we three Marys were there for, to respond to the apparent triumph of darkness over light with bitterness, with obstinacy and rebellion? No. No, it wasn't like that. He died . . . like a king some said afterwards, but what earthly king would die forgiving his killers, caring for a thief as well as for his mother? Because of his actions, his bearing, the way he was, the moment of greatest darkness became the moment when I began to sense, despite the evidence of my eyes, the triumph of his light. I say 'began' because all of us remained bewildered, even after we'd seen him risen from the dead, even after his ascension into heaven when I, together with my other sons and 11 of Jesus' closest friends, came together in that upstairs room to pray.

Often I've thought back to 'the first mother' as she's described in the legends of our tribe. God spoke hope even as he censured her rebellion, saying to the tempting serpent, 'I will put enmity between you and the woman, and between your offspring and hers, he will crush your head and you will strike his heel.' I've come to see that it wasn't the power of goodness which was crushed to death on the cross that day, but the power of evil and of death itself.

And what of me? In that ancient legend, to the woman known as 'Eve' or 'mother of all the living' God said, 'I will greatly increase your pains in the bringing up of children.' Yes, Jesus brought me, his mother, much darkness and pain. I could so easily have failed him. Yet weak as any three lone women in a mob-filled night, we three Marys stood our ground, refusing to hide our tiny, oil-starved lamps under dark cloths of bitterness or rebellion. We played our part, and suddenly were witnessing the dawn of a new light which had never before been seen on this earth. I'm old now; I haven't long here. I've seen my son, God's Son, risen. I belong in a place where his face shines bright as a cloudless, night-less sun.

(Imagined from John 19.25–30)

Whatever your 'name' – your history, background, personality, circumstances – are you turning your face towards darkness, or light?

Abandonment to reconciliation

Fourth Sunday in Lent

[He sent me to] provide for those who grieve in Zion –
to bestow on them a crown of beauty
instead of ashes,
the oil of gladness
instead of mourning,
and a garment of praise
instead of a spirit of despair.
They will be called oaks of righteousness,
a planting of the LORD
for the display of his splendour.

(Isaiah 61.3)

These words are about reversing the shame of abandonment.
Isaiah had prophesied that God's people, ignominiously defeated in battle, would be carted off into exile. Israel had strayed
from God's ways so often. His punishment wasn't intended to
be vindictive, but to bring them to their senses. Afterwards,
God would run to restore his relationship with them.

Not all shame derives from guilt as theirs did, yet the pit of
despair in which it lands people is just as real. God's anointed
one holds out a crown of beauty to any who will take it in
exchange for the ashes of mourning. For garments rent in despair he offers bright clothes of praise. Where they appeared to
bring shame on him (what kind of god lets his people be exiled
far from their worship place?) they will be planted like mighty
oaks, displaying God's splendour as their behaviour changes
from rebellion to righteousness.

With shame, so much comes down to attitude – the way we're facing or leaning. If someone tells me continually that I'm no good, a failure, a horrible person, I'm likely to become those things. But God always has something different to say. He sees that we need to change, for no one is perfect; but he also sees and praises the goodness within us. He sees us as the people he created and loves, he finds us lovable!

* * *

Young student Lucy-May Johnson has experience of God touching the shame in her life. She writes here of how he has helped her to deny its power over her by gradually accepting his very different view of her instead.

When I was 12 I sang a song in front of my class. The whole way through my teacher and peers laughed at me. From that moment on my confidence hit rock bottom. I didn't have any friends at school so I was called a loner. To make matters worse, I tried to make friends with girls, so I was called a lesbian.

I tried to console myself by saying that I had a friend in Jesus, but even then, found attempts to make friends hard. I couldn't open up to anyone but there were peers who I could at least try to talk with. A few years later one of these peers committed suicide.

My first thought was that it should have been me.

At the end of the year, on a Christian camp, I had to read in front of others. Later I shared with someone I trusted how hard it was and he showed me a Bible passage – 1 Peter 1.3–9. It talks about a living hope, something which I never had.

As the years went on I became friends with Christians which, along with smiles and hugs, encouraged me. That, together with those special words from the Bible, began to fill up the empty hole inside me.

Sometimes life throws hard situations at us. We experience emptiness, loss and insecurity, feel alone, isolated and abandoned. It comforts me then to know that it is really true that God loves us for who we are. He made each one of us special, out of his image, by his hand. If tough times face me now I hold on to the truth from John 3.16: 'God so loved the world that he gave his only Son, that whoever believes in him shall not perish but have eternal life.' It helps me to know and to believe that in my heart.

> Aconites come first: green ruffs, unfolding,
> gild winter with sunshine.
> Snowdrops purify the short, dim days.
>
> As you set flowers to prime our faith,
> will you dig and enrich
> the tired, bare earth of our lives, Lord?
>
> Colour our bleakness with green, white, gold;
> live your miracles again in us.
> Christ is risen. He is risen indeed.

You might like to meditate on what it means to find a living hope, through the resurrection of Jesus Christ from the dead.

Monday

While he was still a long way off, his father saw him and was filled with compassion for him; he ran to his son, threw his arms around him and kissed him. The son said to him, 'Father, I have sinned against heaven and against you. I am no longer worthy to be called your son.' But the father said to his servants, 'Quick! Bring the best robe and put it on him. Put a ring on his finger and sandals on his feet. Bring the fattened calf and kill it. Let's have a feast and celebrate. For this son of mine was dead and is alive again; he was lost and is found.' So they began to celebrate.

(Luke 15.20–4 – but do read the whole of Luke 15)

A familiar story, but have you ever stopped to consider how shocking it is?

- It was unheard of for a younger son to take his inheritance and go; in that culture it meant he wished his father dead.
- Fathers, especially those of the age and social standing Jesus indicated, were dignified figures who under no circumstances would hitch up their robes to run.
- Jesus told the stories of the lost coin, sheep and son in response to religious leaders' disapproving mutterings that he partied with sinners. Religious Jews were taught to steer well clear of reprobates lest they be corrupted.
- Each 'lost' story ends with a meal – a disproportionately generous, all-inclusive and 'unfair' party.

Jesus' actions as well as his stories flew in the face of accepted understanding of God's nature, especially of his grace which isn't, in the least, fair. The son who abandoned his father, against all the odds, is reconciled. The son who dutifully stayed behind, working for his father is, where the story ends, lost. Having excluded himself from the celebrations, he has some bridges of pride and resentment to burn. 'I always feel so sorry for him,' someone commented the other day. I used to, until I saw that he'd never really got to know his father who told him, 'Everything I have is yours.' He could have had a close relationship with Dad – and a party any time he wanted. But, as with the religious Jews, duty had taken the place of relationship and he'd lost sight of the father's love amid all the work he was trying to do for him.

Abandonment of parents by children (or vice versa) carries such pain that forgiveness and reconciliation don't come cheap or easy. Maybe there's a degree of rapprochement but relationships remain strained, not what they once were. There may well be jealous repercussions involving siblings. Forgiveness has to be big enough to risk further hurt.

* * *

Born in Barbados, Dr Elaine Arnold has spent years researching the effects when mothers and children, separated through immigration, are reunited. Her varied career has included social work in several London boroughs, co-ordinating mental-health services in Trinidad and Tobago, lecturing in child observation at Sussex University and directing training for the Nafsiyat Intercultural Training Centre.

Elaine watched little ones clinging to adults, any adults, in the large Trinidadian orphanage where she worked in the early 1950s. By no means all of these children were orphans, she knew. Many of their mothers had left their children either there or with relatives, to join the children's fathers who were already seeking a better life in the UK. 'It would only be for a little while,' they said.

Elaine changed career from teaching to social work and, while training in the UK, became interested in the work of Dr John Bowlby. His observations of children during the Second World War showed how desperately they needed a continuing relationship with one person. Years later, back in the UK, Elaine started talking with mothers who had sent for children they had left behind previously in the Caribbean. After an average absence of seven years, they no longer felt the children belonged to them in the same way as children born to them in the UK.

Elaine started working with a group of women who felt they had been abandoned in this way as children. They had sought counselling because they could not trust people and found relationships unsustainable. She let them tell their stories – of arriving, aged around 11 to 13, in the UK. Their mothers were strangers who didn't run to meet them but stood there frozen, looking at them.

Some of these children were able to adapt to their new country and family, just enough to get by. Many were bullied at school because of their 'foreignness' and struggled at home, feeling mere 'child-minders' to the younger siblings their parents preferred. Most arrived with a strong Christian faith and hope, only to find that established churches in the 'Christian Mother Country' rejected them because of their colour. Many later joined black churches where they found strength and nurturing – effectively a new family. Nearly all left their mother's home at the earliest opportunity, settling as far away as possible.

Through counselling, several have come to see that their mothers thought they were doing the best thing, that they hadn't been abandoned from lack of love or care. Reconciled, they care for mothers who are getting older, but still don't confide in or have an easy relationship with them. Some have been unable to show affection and warmth to their own children, which means the damage is passed down to the next generation. On the other hand, after a shaky start, a good number have done well in people-centred careers such as social work or counselling.

Elaine continues to run her 'Separation and Reunion Forum' for these people and longs to see deeper relationships re-established before the older generation dies. When I asked if she ever became discouraged she smiled, 'God helps me.'

Pray for those who, like Elaine, seek to bring reconciliation. And look again at the story of the two sons, particularly the older one, asking God if we've really understood what it is about. For example, are people arriving in your church, your family, rejected and abandoned . . . or received with joy?

Tuesday

The LORD comforts his people
and will have compassion on his afflicted ones.
But Zion said, 'The LORD has forsaken me,
the LORD has forgotten me.'

'Can a mother forget the baby at her breast
and have no compassion on the child she has borne?
Though she may forget,
I will not forget you!
See, I have engraved you on the palms of my hands;
your walls are ever before me.'

(Isaiah 49.13–16)

When things go wrong and I get depressed, sometimes I feel God's tangible comfort. At other times I've felt . . . simply abandoned. Clearly he's gone away, just when I need him. Invariably the church service that Sunday morning turns out to be one long paean of praise to God who is always so loving and faithful and kind. 'Except to me, of course,' I mutter, darkly, convinced that I'm the only one who ever feels this way. Either I've done something awful to chase God away or he's not all he's cracked up to be.

Actually the Psalms are full of cries of those who feel that God has abandoned them. In those days worshippers expressed what they felt, really felt. Whether or not their trouble was of their own making, there is often a jump, a kind of wordless space in the Psalmist's writing, where God meets him and his complaint transforms into an outpouring of praise and love. In this passage in Isaiah, the nation had experienced the punishment of exile; but their bitterness turns as they understand it was the only way God could restore them to himself. As I've found out from many people while writing this book, no matter how abandoned we feel, or for what reason, God is willing and able to find us.

Sadly, the people we love may abandon us. Sometimes that's intentional – a severing of a friendship, an acrimonious divorce, a parent who walks out on his or her family. Even unintentional abandonment, such as the death or mental illness of a loved one, can make us feel angry as well as abandoned. Life may simply move on: a daughter marries a man who lives on the other side of the world. She doesn't lose touch, but things aren't the same. A close friend's work causes him to move away or simply gobbles up the time for shared talk and activities which have been so special.

I guess at such times we have a choice. Either, in our hurt, we sink into a spiral of misery, forgetting those who love or have loved us and concluding that God has abandoned us too. Been there, done that! Or we believe in God, hoping in the only one who has known us since before our birth and who will still know us after our death, the one who has promised he will be faithful and won't forget us.

* * *

Ken Ramsay had a good childhood in many ways. But a fine education at boarding school and a large house in the country in which to enjoy the freedom of the holidays didn't make up for the darker side of home life.

One day, when his father and the man next door arranged to take Ken on a cycle-ride, Ken felt so grown up and recognized. The sun was shining on the primroses in the narrow country lanes, the birds were singing. The following week he offered to mow next door's lawn, enjoying the experience of being kind to someone who had reached out to him. But one look at his mother's face when she came across him cleaning the mower afterwards told him something was very wrong. He learned that his mother had fallen out with the neighbours and felt that Ken had created a problem. His childish impulse to help others came under strain. His mother meant well but she had ongoing emotional difficulties and later Ken was devastated when she told him, 'I could never – can never – love you.'

What we learn as children goes deep. Psychologically speaking, lack of love often passes down the generations. Ken finished his schooling, joined the army and, on his discharge after the war, went in search of girls. One of his army mates assured him a good source was Lee Abbey in Devon. There Ken found his girl. He says, with a twinkle in his eye, that he 'very sensibly ran off with their cook', and he's still married to Val, 50-odd years later. But first in the Christian community of Lee Abbey he found God, and God gave him a love for people which he would never have believed possible. Ken became ordained in the Anglican Church and embarked on an unusual but truly people-centred ministry. For years he and Val lived in various Christian communities, embracing the challenge of getting on with all kinds of folk. He also served as a worker-priest, drawing alongside colleagues in several factories.

Ken and Val are close to their two children and to their grand-children. So many other people love him too. I mentioned his name once and a woman's face lit up. 'Do you know him? Ken's a real saint!' she said. 'I was widowed a couple of years ago and, somehow, at those moments when everything seemed dark and hopeless, that's exactly when Ken would phone. I don't know how he knew, but he always had just the right words and made me feel so much better.'

Deprived of the love of his mother, found by God, gifted with love for others – that's Ken!

Meditate on St Paul's soaring poetry in Romans 8.38–9 – and ask God what it means that nothing can separate us from his love. Picture your name, and the names of those you love, not just pencilled, but engraved, on the palms of his hands.

Wednesday

My God, my God, why have you forsaken me?
Why are you so far from saving me,
so far from the words of my groaning? . . .
In you our fathers put their trust;
they trusted and you delivered them . . .

But I am a worm and not a man,
scorned by men and despised by the people.
All who see me mock me;
they hurl insults, shaking their heads:
'He trusts in the LORD;
let the LORD rescue him.
Let him deliver him,
since he delights in him.' . . .
I am poured out like water,
and all my bones are out of joint.
My heart has turned to wax;
it has melted away within me.
My strength is dried up like a potsherd,
and my tongue sticks to the roof of my mouth;
you lay me in the dust of death.
Dogs have surrounded me;
a band of evil men has encircled me,
they have pierced my hands and my feet.
I can count all my bones;
people stare and gloat over me.
They divide my garments among them
and cast lots for my clothing.
But you, O LORD, be not far off;
O my Strength, come quickly to help me.

(Psalm 22.1, 4, 6–8, 14–19)

This Psalm prefigures so many details of Jesus' death: the terrible physical pain of crucifixion and the mental anguish of seeing the very people he had come to save turn on him. Surely the worst pain was spiritual as, for the first time in eternity, he became cut off from his close, loving relationship with his Father and cried out in a loud voice the Psalm's opening words, 'My God, my God, why have you forsaken me?' (Matthew 27.46). Imagine the contrast as Jesus was vindicated, restored, glorified, rejoiced over that first Easter!

If ever I feel in some small way 'abandoned', like the Psalmist I find it hard to accept God's promises. In a cold and painful place they can seem but empty words. Yet in time I come to realize that even if I fail to hold on to him, he holds on to me, meets me in the 'tomb', if you like. Recently I was talking with a friend who has been supporting a young mum whose husband has gone off with another woman. She's coping not only with their two small children but with the added anguish of his threats and aggression. 'It's been such a difficult time for her,' my friend remarked, 'but she's always saying, "I don't know how I'd get through this without God!" and telling me another story of some everyday way in which he's helped her. She's thanked me for being there for her but to me she's a real inspiration.' This woman was only just finding out about Christianity and beginning to get to know God when her husband left. Is that an Easter I glimpse emerging from her particular Good Friday?

* * *

Sometimes the pain of abandonment leads to a desperate heart-cry which reaches God's ears, even though, at the time, the person has no understanding of God, let alone of prayer. That's what I felt when talking to Jeanne Flynn, who tells her story here.

> 'She has spina bifida, hydrocephalus and a mild form of spasticity.' That's what the doctors told my mum when I was born in the 1950s. They said I'd be a 'living cabbage', mentally and physically incapable from the neck down. 'Put her in a home, forget about her and have another child,' they advised. 'She'll probably be dead in six days anyway.' Then another hospital packed the nerve endings back into my spine. If I survived I might make 30, they predicted. I'm now 47.

Mum had also prepared herself for my death. Her family has a history of mental illness and when they handed me back to her she developed severe post-natal depression. With my father in prison, my grandparents helped care for me; then they went to live abroad. Aged two to four I lived in a children's home and then was fostered for three terrible years. I remember no food there, except for sweeties and Sunday lunch, I had no education, no physio and my foster mother convinced the authorities I was mentally retarded because I couldn't tie my shoelaces.

My grandparents found out what was going on when they returned from New Zealand. They took me to live with them. I didn't see my mother until I was nearly nine. She turned up with a beautiful French doll. I tore its head off and yelled that I didn't want another mother. I went to a special needs boarding school from age ten but couldn't cope with people. I'd go so berserk that doctors kept me on Valium until I was 26. I had no friends. One girl at school kept a photo of her happy-looking family by her bedside. I smashed it over her head. But I do remember singing about houses built on rock and on sand and acknowledging that God somehow existed beyond my world. People like ministers, nuns and Sunday school teachers made me feel safe – not that they'd have known it. I was horrid to them.

When I reached 16 and went to live and work at a centre for people with disabilities I was still verbally violent – and physically too, so far as I was able. Things began to change when Joan Keating, a local preacher who lived in the village, came to the centre, initially to teach me to read and write. Soon she became my friend, despite my hurling all kinds of abuse at her. Joan has counselling experience and helped me to talk through things which had happened. She treated me as part of her family. She would take me to churches where she was preaching too. It was no quick investment which she and her husband made in me. Not until I was 35 was I confident even to allow people to say 'Good morning' to me. Before that I used to blank them off or shut them up.

Later I experienced a good measure of physical healing when someone prayed for me at a Christian meeting, though recently a stoma prolapsed and now I'm confined to a special bed or electric wheelchair. But to be honest I'm not that worried. What's more important is that I'm free to be me – to love God, to love people, to relate to them, even to help them. And you know, all the people in my family who were so messed up could have had that love and freedom too!

A recently widowed friend gave me an image which I've found helpful. In a time of transition, when you may feel abandoned, cold and alone in a pain-filled 'tomb', it's easy to try to find a solution with which you feel comfortable, which seems to fit you. But it will probably be the wrong solution, for this is a time of waiting, waiting for God. And he, who knows you better than you know yourself, may well have something altogether different (and better) in mind.

Thursday

Have mercy on me, O God, have mercy on me,
for in you my soul takes refuge.
I will take refuge in the shadow of your wings
until the disaster has passed.
I cry out to God Most High,
to God, who fulfils his purpose for me . . .
My heart is steadfast, O God,
my heart is steadfast;
I will sing and make music.
Awake, my soul!
Awake, harp and lyre!
I will awaken the dawn . . .
For great is your love, reaching to the heavens;
your faithfulness reaches to the skies.

(Psalm 57.1–2, 7–8, 10)

The Psalmist certainly found himself abandoned: 'I am in the midst of lions; I lie among ravenous beasts – men whose teeth are spears and arrows, whose tongues are sharp swords' (verse 4). When he cried to God, rescue appeared to come quite quickly. For others it's far less dramatic but more drawn out. That may well be harder. For example, I know so many Christians, mainly women, who are married to someone who doesn't share their relationship with God. That can come to feel like a kind of abandonment of a loved and loving spouse who can't share this fundamental of your life. Conflicting loyalties when it comes to family decisions or to time spent with God and other Christians, can carry an oppressive weight of guilt. The thought of dying, with the possibility of separate eternities, is hard to bear.

Shivering slightly, I watched a September day dawn over the Adriatic recently. Black night, then the faintest colours, deepening, lightening, washing sky and sea, revealing more of the land. And then the moment when, 'ping!', the sun appeared over the blue mountain on the horizon, in token of the warm, perfect day to come.

How can we 'sing' to 'awaken the dawn'? Doing so in a literal sense would hardly improve a marital situation! But there's truth embedded in this Psalm about the steadfast heart which, knowing God, remains full of faith, hope and praise, making the kind of sounds which allow God's grace to work in the situation. The timing may not be to our liking. It may take years, not hours, but some day God's love will dawn on the person.

* * *

Allan, a retired special-needs teacher, had no idea he was lost until after he was found. For years he'd simply felt a bit . . .

jealous. Until a funny thing happened on the way to the Jordan. He told me:

When I fell in love with Barbara 40 years ago, I felt a little jealous. She had something that I didn't: her Christian faith was clearly central to her. But I'm an honest person of scientific bent – and Jesus couldn't still be alive! I married Barbara and went to church with her wherever we lived. Always open about my non-belief, I wouldn't pray, say the Creed or take Communion but enjoyed singing at church and liked the people. They became our friends. They accepted me, even got me reading the Bible in the services or acting in a drama group. Once, during a rehearsal, we were asked to pray out loud for the person on our right. Not knowing how to handle that, I said, 'My mum told me never to talk to strange people and you're a stranger to me, God.' More hurtful was when one of our own kids, aged six, asked why I wouldn't pray with him at night.

Thirteen years ago I went with Barbara to a huge Christian conference called Spring Harvest. They held special seminars for agnostics. One speaker called Gerald Coates told us about some things he was sorry for in his life. I was sorry for many things too, so I was with him all the way until he asked all the men who were believing Christians to stand and say, 'Sorry!' I felt left out, almost jealous again. When he asked those who didn't believe to do the same, uncharacteristically I stood up and shot forward, weeping. At the same conference, a brilliant South African cosmologist called Louw Alberts helped me resolve some scientific doubts about religion; he convinced me that the universe must have been designed, couldn't have 'just happened'.

Five years later Barbara and I went on a trip to Israel. Led by a clergy friend whose church we'd attended when we lived in Merseyside, we 'did' the southern biblical sites at breakneck speed. It was only in Galilee, when the pace slowed a little, that all I'd heard about Jesus suddenly made sense. He was who he said he was! The minister had no idea when he cracked a joke at supper: 'We're off to the River Jordan tomorrow. Good place to get baptized, Allan!'

I hardly slept that night. I woke Barbara to say that I thought all my questions about Jesus being alive had been answered and what did she think? 'You must make up your own mind,' she muttered, sleepily. 'We've discussed it so many times before.' Later, as she showered, I packed a towel and spare clothes in our day-bag. Passing the minister's table on the way in to breakfast I asked, 'Were you serious about baptizing me?'

He laughed. 'No, of course not!' Then he saw my face. Barbara, sitting at another table, thought I'd told a funny story when everyone at the minister's table erupted in wild whoops and wails. A dramatic surprise awaited her at the Jordan. She found herself wading in with me and the minister.

Back home a friend of ours was reading the lesson when she caught sight of me and had to stop. It was quite a job after that, restoring the service to order. Blame my T-shirt: it said, 'I've been baptized in the River Jordan'.

Pray for peace, wisdom and grace for all those whose spouses or families don't share their trust in God, and for his love to dawn on those they love.

Friday

'Therefore I am now going to allure her;
I will lead her into the desert
and speak tenderly to her.
There I will give her back her vineyards,
and will make the Valley of Achor a door of hope.
There she will sing as in the days of her youth,
as in the day she came up out of Egypt.
In that day,' declares the LORD, 'you will call me "my husband";
you will no longer call me "my master".'

(Hosea 2.14–16)

I love this tale of resurrection and grace. A man named Achan, back in Joshua 7, had disobeyed God so strikingly that he was stoned to death in the valley thereafter named 'Achor', which means 'trouble'. Once again, in Hosea's time, God had been punishing Israel for running after false gods. This 'leading her into the wilderness' was not for retribution. God wanted to restore the relationship, to find Israel again in the wilderness, have her fall in love with him all over again. He longed for her to know his love, his goodness as a bride, rather than his harsh discipline as a slave. The valley of trouble will become a door of hope.

I haven't often been lost or felt abandoned, but when I have, I've been very anxious to be found straight away. In the meanwhile it's tempting to think that God is lost too, or, more likely, that he's lost any interest in me. That is never true. If you read the rest of Hosea you catch a glimpse of God's love and the lengths to which he's prepared to go. He's with us when we can't see or feel him. He's with us when all others seem to have abandoned us, along with any hope which we once had. He's never given up on us even though we may never know the reason why we had to wait.

* * *

A retired surveyor told me his story of being abandoned . . . and not reconciled, but found.

> Christopher walked back from work that day with no idea that anything was wrong. In his family home he found one chair, the television set and nothing else. No food, no bed, no car. Worse still he had no idea where his wife and two children, a boy and a girl aged eight and nine, might be. He sat on the empty hall floor and wailed.
>
> Christopher had thought his ten-year marriage to Kay as happy as anyone's. But when the phone rang a few hours later – 'I've

89

bought a house the other side of town and I'm living there with the children now' – he knew her mind was fixed and nothing he could say would bring her home.

Later Christopher learned that his family were living in a squalid property over a shop, along with his wife's lover. It turned out Kay had been seeing this particular man for two years and having numerous affairs before that.

A few weeks after his family left, urgent ringing on the doorbell woke Christopher at two in the morning. He could hear his wife crying and rushed to open the front door, but a giant of a man towered over him.

'Is that you, you bastard?' his wife's friend yelled, before punching small, inoffensive Christopher on the nose, knocking him out. When Christopher came to, there was blood all over the floor and the man was kicking him, breaking one of his ribs. Christopher hauled himself painfully to his feet, stood with blood streaming down his face and found himself saying, 'I'm sure we can find a way around this. Why not come in for a cup of tea?'

Blind-drunk, the man raged, 'You, you, you . . .' Finally he found the worst insult in his vocabulary, 'You pen-pusher, you!' The glass broke as the front door slammed behind him.

Christopher could hardly believe what had happened. More desolate than ever, abused and abandoned in his own home, he arrived at work the next morning still in shock and asked if he could have some time off to report the incident to the police. The Chief Executive of the Council where he worked seemed devoid of compassion. 'If you must – but come straight back!'

The police weren't much better. 'If you press charges we can't guarantee this man won't harm your children.'

Christopher's only real support for the next eight years was his father. They would get together every weekend and Christopher respected him greatly, but the old man's worsening Parkinson's Disease meant he needed an increasing amount of care. Finally, he was admitted to hospital, his mind gone. A few weeks later, Christopher sat at his dying father's side, thinking there really was nothing left now, when in walked a gorgeous Norwegian woman. Inger explained that she'd been a patient of his dentist-father for years. He'd been a good friend to her. Hearing that he was dying, she'd come to say goodbye.

Today Christopher isn't bitter or lonely. He believes his experiences made him a better, stronger person. 'I'd built a castle around myself in my first marriage,' he said. 'One of the reasons Kay broke away was that I'd been over-controlling, but now I'm free.' Proof of that perhaps is that Inger and Christopher have been happily married for 25 years.

After I'd talked with Christopher, Inger, beaming, handed me a poem she'd just written, her first ever – an outpouring of praise to the God she knows is faithful through all the seasons of life. Whichever season you're in, let God speak to you through it.

Majesty
I am the seasons.
The seasons are me.
Spring is me.
Summer is me.
Autumn is me.
Winter is me.
Who am I?
I am the joy in you
That makes everything new.
I am the love
That makes all things grow –
The trees and flowers
New and old.
All the beauty you see
Is also me.
Spring is me.
Summer is me.

Autumn is me.
Winter is me.
I am the seasons.
The seasons are me.

Saturday

Crucified

Another week, another mother. You'll not have heard of me. I don't get a mention in your Scriptures, and why should I? My boy wasn't the Saviour, wasn't the good one. Had every chance of course, but what can you do in the end? Nice Jewish boy, gone to the dogs, becomes a common thief. It happens. It hurts. Hurts the victims, hurts the mothers more. And the fathers, except my son's father was dead by then. As for our son, he deserved punishment, yes. According to our law he deserved death, by stoning. Crucifixion? No, no one deserves that!

'Course I couldn't save him. I didn't abandon him though. I was there, saw him die. And, before him, the other one, the one who had been famous and would be again. I saw him die as well. His mother was there, plus one of his friends and a few women. But all the others who'd been cheering him on, great crowds of them, where were they? There were crowds all right, not cheering but jeering – a foul-mouthed lot, taunting, 'God would rescue you if he loved you.' I could understand the Romans. They were warning off any more troublesome 'Messiahs'. They were mocking us too by putting up a notice above a beaten, dying man on a cross announcing, 'Here's the king of the Jews'. What got me though . . . it was our own religious leaders who handed him over to the Romans. Begged them to crucify him. And what had he done wrong? That's what my son said when he was hanging on that cross. 'We are getting what we deserve, but this man has

done nothing wrong.' I'd been squirming with shame to see my boy on that gibbet, but you know, when he said those words I was proud of him. Yes, proud, for the first time in years!

And then he turned to Jesus, asked him to remember him when he came into his Kingdom. Tell me how a thief saw that Jesus was King when no one else could? Four hours before he died, strung up on a cross, he found Jesus. And Jesus found him. I heard his reply, 'I tell you the truth, today you will be with me in paradise.'

Me? My husband left me when he died. My son left me when he started his lying and thieving ways – and then he, too, died. But, you know what? I found Jesus that day, though by the time I did, he too was dead. 'Dead and gone,' they say. Except he wasn't, not Jesus. He's the only one who's never left me.

(Imagined from Luke 23.32–43)

Remember any times when you abandoned God and he found you.

Blindness or unbelief to faith

Fifth Sunday in Lent

They will be called oaks of righteousness,
a planting of the LORD
for the display of his splendour.

(Isaiah 61.3)

Who will be called oaks of righteousness? Who will be planted
by God to display his splendour? The poor, the broken-hearted,
captives and prisoners, those who mourned or were in despair.
Well, really! What kind of god wants those kinds of people?
We may find it uncomfortable but still the answer is . . . our
kind of God!

We may not see any viable life, let alone great oaks of righteousness, in such storm-tossed, shattered timbers. But God
does. The whole Bible, the whole of Jesus' ministry, points to
his giving far more attention to those kinds of people than
to the rich, the successful, the neat and tidy, the ones who
think they've got it all right. I know I have blindness, people-
blindness, and the kind of unbelief that, deep down, assumes
God can't touch people with profound mental problems, or
won't change things for those who've been stuck at the bottom
of the heap for decades – to take just two examples.

The thing is, people don't become perfect overnight, or
ever, in this life. Judah, to whom these words refer, certainly
didn't come back from exile totally reformed, living justly,
seeking mercy and walking humbly with their God. The early
Church – was that any better? Hardly. Paul's letters reveal

individuals and churches bringing God's name into disrepute all over the place. Take me and you: aren't we the same mixture of God-rooted goodness and the opposite? God relies on imperfect people to display his splendour. Oaks of righteousness sound so solid, so dependable. It makes me humble. I imagine that's what God intends.

* * *

Recently I led a creative writing week, within a Christian context. For some reason, this time an unusually high proportion of those attending had mental-health issues. I lack skills to meet such needs. Some wrote little, if anything, yet something better happened. We saw God's invisible, upside-down Kingdom become visible as, 'damaged' or 'normal', everyone helped each other. Everyone had something to give. Ages ranged from 18 to 86; several different first languages and physical disabilities could have erected further barriers, yet never have I known a group so inclusive. Not all called themselves Christians, many had very difficult lives, but each one reflected something of God's splendour. My faith and my hope grew because of it.

As Senior Vice President of a successful computer company, English businessman Tony Cotterill was enjoying life in the States and had little time for people who couldn't help themselves. Meanwhile his wife, Sue, unable to obtain a work permit there, helped in a voluntary capacity with a group of people who had mental-health or learning difficulties. Sue had become a Christian some years before and her church in the States gathered the group once a month for a meal. She asked Tony to help out one Sunday afternoon. Initially he thought, 'What a nice guy I am to help those poor people.' Later, to his surprise, he found himself wondering who had gained most from the experience and concluded it had to be himself. He'd put such store by money and position, but were they important in the final analysis? Who, on his deathbed, wishes he'd spent more time at the office? No, Tony realized that he was no better than people he'd previously pitied and, in his mind, marginalized. He could see that they had so much to offer. 'They became a key part of my four-year search for God,' Tony said.

Company changes took Tony and Sue back to England. Sue found a job with a National Health Trust, which again involved running clubs for people with learning difficulties, while Tony, having become a Christian himself, threw himself into a lively Anglican church. He led Alpha courses and men's ministry. He preached. He busied himself with church activities nearly every night of the week. He even considered becoming ordained but concluded that God wanted him to remain in business.

One Sunday morning, on his way to church as usual, Tony found himself inexplicably going the wrong way and driving to a different church. He'd been there before but had felt he'd little in common with the people there. 'I don't know why I'm here,' he confessed that morning to the minister, John Berry.

'I think I know,' said John. He explained how his church kept attracting people in need. They stayed because they felt accepted and at home. Should the church be reaching out to the needy in a more organized way? They aren't a large congregation, per-haps 50 to 70, yet they had already decided to fund the employ-ment of a full-time pastoral worker with psychological and nursing skills. Now they needed to raise £16,000 for her second year.

'I have the counselling skills of a brick,' laughed Tony, 'but I know about selling and how to organize and present a business plan and that could prove helpful alongside John's pastor's heart and love of people.'

Tony has come to see that in many ways we're all afflicted, we all have our foibles; you could say that we're all mentally ill to some degree. So who are we to play God and decide who is and who is not beyond 'normality'? 'If we can see people for who they are – men and women with much to offer – we can provide

96

stepping-stones and build confidence, give encouragement, practical help and share facilities,' Tony said. 'It's amazing what changes can happen. There are so many people who want to help but don't know how, so many under-used resources, such as churches and school buildings. Bring those together, give some training and support – and people who are marginalized now could become net givers into the community again.'

Tony has joined John and others in the process of defining an 'Integrated Support Organization' with churches and other organizations in their town. Currently called 'Project 61', the organization has Isaiah, Chapter 61 as its inspiration. It should give hope and belief not only to those it is helping. Judging by Tony's own experience, the helpers will receive even more.

Astoundingly, God, you put your faith in us. We're part of your plan to turn this world upside-down, so it becomes the right way up, the way you always intended it to be. Show me, God, where I'm blind, where I lack the faith to see your passion for the people I've written off as hopeless cases. Help me see – and act.

Monday

The Son of Man came eating and drinking, and you say, 'Here is a glutton and a drunkard, a friend of tax collectors and "sinners" . . . '

Now one of the Pharisees invited Jesus to have dinner with him . . . When a woman who had lived a sinful life in that town learned that Jesus was eating at the Pharisee's house, she brought an alabaster jar of perfume, and as she stood behind him at his feet weeping, she began to wet his feet with her tears. Then she wiped them with her hair, kissed them and poured perfume on them. When the Pharisee who had invited him saw this, he said to himself, 'If this man were a prophet, he would know who is touching him and what kind of woman she is – that she is a sinner.' . . . Then [Jesus] turned towards the woman and said to Simon [the Pharisee], 'Do you see this woman? I came into your house. You did not give me any water for my feet, but she wet my feet with her tears and wiped them with her hair. You did not give me a kiss, but this woman, from the time I entered, has not stopped kissing my feet. You did not put oil on my head, but she has poured perfume on my feet. Therefore, I tell you, her many sins have been forgiven – for she loved much. But he who has been forgiven little loves little.' Then Jesus said to her, 'Your sins are forgiven.'   (Luke 7.34, 36–9, 44–8)

Who is blind here? Not the woman, who sees Jesus clearly for who he is and expresses her gratitude in the only way she knows. The religious people see what I suspect I might have seen. Come on, a 'woman who had lived a sinful life' performs shockingly intimate 'aromatherapy' on your church leader, weeping and kissing his naked feet, what are you going to think? About her? About him? But Jesus implied that the religious people were blind, explaining the woman's extraordinary behaviour by the example of debtors – which person would love the person who cancelled his debt most, one who owed much or one who owed little? Yes, this upstart young rabbi from the back of beyond was attempting to justify an already shocking incident by the 'blasphemy' that he could forgive sins. Good Jews knew that was God's prerogative alone!

Detaching myself from over-familiarity with this story, I'm afraid I'd have shared the Pharisee's blindness. And then I'm reminded of Isaiah's words, 'Woe to those who call evil good and good evil, who put darkness for light and light for darkness' (Isaiah 5.20).

Who showed faith here? The woman put her faith in Jesus, that he would forgive her sins. She gave him her love. But Jesus also had faith in her – that, remarkably, she had seen him

for who he was and so her love wasn't the inappropriate kind
it appeared to others.

'Friend of sinners'. I've always thought that a lovely title
of Jesus, because we're all sinners, aren't we? But it has its
uncomfortable side. What would the people I respect think if
I did become friends with a thoroughly unrespectable, law-
breaking kind of sinner? Would I want to be his or her friend?
Does our blindness prevent such people from finding faith?

* * *

Most of us aren't good at sharing Jesus' love with those who
don't know him. Do you tell them you can see and they're
blind? Preach at them? Give them something to read, and run?
Mix only with safe, forgiven sinners, in church, hoping, despite the fact it hardly ever happens, that unforgiven ones will
wander into a service and find God?

> John Kerr, at present a housing officer in Inverness, told me
> about the years when he worked for a mission to sea-farers.
> Despite his faithfulness in trying to reach them for Christ, few
> sailors arriving in port after months at sea seemed interested in
> talking about God or in reading tracts or Gospels. John began
> to wonder what good he was doing. A man of prayer, he took
> his doubts to God. Soon he sensed God asking him, 'What did
> they call Jesus?'
>
> 'Friend of sinners.'
>
> 'Well, that's all I'm asking you to be.'
>
> Feeling relieved of a great burden, John stopped trying
> to preach and give out literature and instead did all he could to
> be a practical friend to these men. Some called regularly at the
> port, others came only once but word got around that John
> would help them, even getting up in the middle of the night to
> put a call through to someone they loved on the other side of
> the world. The mission was somewhere warm to sit and drink
> tea and to sort out all kinds of practicalities, but steering

conversation towards spiritual matters still proved a real turn-off. Some of these men must have spiritual needs, though, thought John. He started asking God, 'Is there anyone in particular I should talk to?' He found that, some days, God would direct his thoughts and prayers towards one individual. 'If I'd have gone crashing in, talking about God in front of that sailor's mates, he'd have done a runner out of sheer embarrassment,' John said. So he would pray silently that the other men would leave the room – and watch in wonder as, one by one, they did. Then he found he could talk easily and naturally with the sailor God had pointed out, maybe even pray with him. The results weren't spectacular, he didn't convert all of the world's merchant navies but, 'I tell you, relaxing and letting God do the work was a lot more effective than all my previous efforts.'

Lord, when it comes to helping others find faith in you, I'm often frighteningly blind. But you have 20/20 vision. Help me see others through your eyes. Help me to follow you in being a genuine friend of sinners.

Tuesday

'Do not worry about your life, what you will eat or drink; or about your body, what you will wear. Is not life more important than food, and the body more important than clothes? . . . See how the lilies of the field grow. They do not labour or spin. Yet I tell you that not even Solomon in all his splendour was dressed like one of these. If that is how God clothes the grass of the field, which is here today and tomorrow is thrown into the fire, will he not much more clothe you, O you of little faith? So do not worry, saying, "What shall we eat?" or "What shall we drink?" or "What shall we wear?" For the pagans run after all these things, and your heavenly Father knows that you need them. But seek first his kingdom and his righteousness, and all these things will be given to you as well. Therefore do not worry about

tomorrow, for tomorrow will worry about itself. Each day has
enough trouble of its own.'   (Matthew 6.25–34)

We may say cheerfully, 'Oh yes, I believe in God', but, if little
things encourage us, little things also catch us out. I spend
more time worrying about them than I do praying, and more
time praying panicky little prayers than I do praising God. Yet
people who instead spend time in companionship with him,
enjoying the life and nourishment he's given them, often seem,
like the flowers of the field, to grow ever more beautiful.

I wonder what kind of flowers Jesus had in mind? Thyme
would be good. On our local chalk-downs, thyme releases a
wonderful perfume when bruised underfoot – and then springs
back, hardy as anything. I prickle and create no-go areas, like a
spiky thistle. What makes me do this? Worry, especially when
I feel things are out of control.

This morning I woke up extremely worried because I was
stranded far from home. My car had disappeared. In fact it
was looking increasingly as if it had been stolen from the service station where I'd left it to be repaired and people there
seemed too busy to be bothered. It took me a few minutes to
realize that none of this was true. Actually I was in my bed at
home. I have no plans to drive more than a few miles in the
foreseeable future. My car is locked up safely a few yards away
in our own garage and it doesn't need repairing. Ridiculous,
isn't it, this mind-set which makes me dream up worrying
situations even in my sleep? A real drain of energy, of imagination, frittering away the resurrection power which ushers in
the Kingdom of God. If I put his Kingdom first, if Jesus really
was the centre of my life, I wouldn't worry so much about my
circumstances, or those of my family, my friends, my church
or my community. God's agenda would come first. Maybe I'd
dream his dreams!

As it is I'm quite capable of worrying horribly about my worrying – of deciding that I'm a hopeless case. That's sheer blindness and unbelief because, with God, there is no such word as 'hopeless'. Yet, despite all my confessions above, I do have faith in Jesus. Much more amazingly, he continues to have faith in me.

* * *

Val Ramsay is married to a clergyman. She writes about a worrying moment when faith, hope and God's presence came to her in a simple way: God's grace ministered through the flowers of the field.

I was going through a difficult time; we had just moved house when my husband became unwell. Having moved previously many times, we had become adept at working together and arranging the new house to suit us, a creative process which drew us together and made the house feel like home. Now, in a sense, I was on my own. If we were to have a home rather than a muddle and a heap of boxes, I would have to organize it. Where to begin? There was so much to do and I had a sick husband to care for. I felt confused; we had a strong sense that God had guided us in this move, so why were things proving so difficult?

One morning, quite early, I decided to go for a short walk to distance myself from the problems and gain some perspective. It was a glorious May morning, the birds were singing and the countryside was looking perfect. Simply to be out in all that beauty was a healing experience. There was nobody about and I wandered along absorbing the sights, sounds and smells. I noticed many different varieties of tall grasses sparkling with dew. Some had short, stocky seed heads; others were delicate, shaking in the breeze and shimmering in the sunshine. I marvelled at their intricacy, variety and beauty and selected a bunch to take home. As I put them in a vase I felt that my spirits were gently raised and I was infused with new vision and hope. I was reminded of Jesus' teaching on the lilies of the field and how lavishly God clothes them. I thought of how grasses and flowers come up new every season. He would take care of us and things would work out. I was given the faith and hope to believe it.

Most of us have some area where our faith is blind. Can you, like Val, find something which will remind you to believe God before that blind area leads into an unhelpful inner dialogue. For example, I have a fridge magnet which says, 'Attitude changes everything' – and a happy photo of someone I worry about.

Wednesday

As he approached Bethphage and Bethany at the hill called the Mount of Olives, he sent two of his disciples, saying to them, 'Go to the village ahead of you, and as you enter it, you will find a colt tied there, which no one has ever ridden. Untie it and bring it here. If anyone asks you, "Why are you untying it?" tell him, "The Lord needs it."'

Those who were sent ahead went and found it just as he had told them. As they were untying the colt, its owners asked them, 'Why are you untying the colt?'

They replied, 'The Lord needs it.'

They brought it to Jesus, threw their cloaks on the colt and put Jesus on it.   (Luke 19.29–35)

'Think about it,' said the preacher in my church one morning. 'Jesus is just about to undertake his triumphal entry into Jerusalem – one of the main events which upset the authorities and brought about his crucifixion. And here, at this pivotal point in a tightly written story, are a whole eight verses, detailing exactly how the disciples got hold of the animal on which

Jesus rode. Mark's and Luke's Gospels are similar. Why? What is this saying?'

We don't know whether Jesus knew the owner of the colt and had arranged matters with him: after all, he had stayed nearby with Martha, Mary and Lazarus often enough. Maybe God gave Jesus instructions about the colt, which he passed on to his disciples. Either way, Jesus told his friends what to do and say, they obeyed, and he had a colt to ride. Was this story recorded to show the learning process the disciples were going through? Do something simple, get it right, and you're ready to do something slightly more complex. It works when you're teaching a child or adult to do something practical; perhaps it works when learning faith, hope and trust. Do this odd thing of untying someone else's colt and taking it away. Find that the owner doesn't hit you or shout 'Stop thief!' but lets you proceed. When Jesus asks you to do something which makes you step a little further out of your comfort zones, maybe you'll be ready to do that too. Hebrews 11.1 says, 'Faith is being sure of what we hope for and certain of what we do not see.' That sounds like a huge demand. My own faith and trust, my spiritual sight, grow most from all the little things where I've seen God prove himself faithful.

* * *

Sister Edna Cole is part of the Servants with Jesus group in Sussex – women who are dedicated to praying for the love and unity of God's people and who, by their praying, living and speaking, seek to lift him up to the world. They have seen God do amazing things, things I might find intimidating, except that Edna and her husband, George, are the kind of Christians who radiate Jesus' love; their faith is quiet and real. I asked Edna for an example from her own life of one of those 'little' faith-builders and she told me of something which happened many years ago.

We had a lot to be thankful for. Our youngest daughter, Christine, had recovered from a successful leg operation and was learning afresh how to walk. But we had spent so much on travelling daily from Sussex to visit her in a London hospital. Christmas was fast approaching and we had hardly any money left for presents. Then we found out that our other daughter longed, with all the passion of a seven-year-old, for a dolls' house, complete with furniture. Christine wanted a doll's pram. How could we possibly afford those things? But then I thought, if God can supply all our needs, that would include presents for two little girls, wouldn't it?

A member of our Bible study group came to the door soon afterwards. Would we like a dolls' house? Her daughter had outgrown hers and they needed the space. I was startled, but delighted!

Then, on Christmas Eve, with a few pounds left in my purse from our monthly pay packet, I journeyed to the toy shop in town. I didn't really expect them to have any doll's prams left, and certainly not at a price we could afford. Yet my heart did trust God and I hoped against hope. As I walked into the shop an assistant was bending over a little doll's pram, placing a sale price on it, exactly the amount I had to spend. What joy it was to discover that God had heard our prayers – and to share with him the thrill and delight at the happiness in our house next morning.

Open our eyes, Lord, to appreciate your 'little' kindnesses towards us, and towards those we love.

Thursday

One of the criminals who hung there hurled insults at him: 'Aren't you the Christ? Save yourself and us!'

> But the other criminal rebuked him. 'Don't you fear God,' he said, 'since you are under the same sentence? We are punished justly, for we are getting what our deeds deserve. But this man has done nothing wrong.'
>
> Then he said, 'Jesus, remember me when you come into your kingdom.'
>
> Jesus answered him, 'I tell you the truth, today you will be with me in paradise.' (Luke 23.39–43)

It took something, didn't it, for a man suffering crucifixion to see that the middle 'criminal' of the three of them had done nothing wrong. And then to see that Jesus wasn't some crazy blasphemer claiming to be God's anointed one. He truly was the Messiah. The thief hadn't much learning or theology, but he saw and believed something amazing: that this bloodied, helpless half-corpse was about to be crowned King. The thief didn't repent (or if he did it's not recorded). He didn't get rescued from the cross. But Jesus said that he would 'be with me', sooner than his resurrection. 'Today' they would meet in paradise. Wherever that is, it's surely not a couple of crosses on a hillside outside Jerusalem.

I've seen an amusing drama sketch where angels, preparing in great excitement for the arrival of the first Christian in heaven, are decidedly put out when this scruffy thief turns up, knowing nothing except that Jesus was special. But then it's always surprising to read in the Gospels exactly who could see Jesus and who was blind.

People are 'converted' from unbelief to faith in many different ways, some of them every bit as dramatic as the thief on the cross. I wonder how many people, for example, have been blinded, as Saul was on the road to Damascus (Acts 9)? And how many, do you think, blame their newfound faith on a dog bite?

* * *

Charlie Bridges had been to Sunday school as a child. By the time they were thinking about marriage, he and his fiancée, Chris, felt a church wedding would be hypocritical, as God meant so little to either of them. Later, Chris wanted their son christened though, and an interview with the Vicar got her thinking. Suddenly Charlie, a down-to-earth carpenter and joiner, found himself with a dead-keen Christian wife.

'She wasn't subtle,' said Charlie. 'I'd wake up in the morning and a little note on the pillow would say "You need God!" It made me cross. I did once sneak a look at her Bible notes when she was out at a church meeting. They meant nothing to me.'

Over the next ten years, Charlie attended a few short courses about the Christian faith, but 'wasn't sold on God'. Finally he told a leader, 'I'm a practical kind of guy. I wouldn't just get in a car, I want to know how it works. All this talking isn't helping. If God's there, he'll have to prove it to me.'

Shortly afterwards, Charlie had a week's work in a house where there was a vicious dog. Everything went well until he returned on the Saturday to finish off. The man of the house, now home from work, didn't realize that the dog had to be shut in the kitchen while Charlie was there. He came out of the kitchen just as Charlie was carrying a door down the stairs. The dog rushed out, bit Charlie on the knee, drawing blood; but, fortunately for Charlie, he was distracted by the door falling on him. Charlie returned home, enjoyed his weekend and started another job on the Monday. On the Tuesday evening his knee was aching and by 2.00 am felt so bad that he went downstairs for a painkiller. He reached the bottom step semi-conscious and shivering. Grabbing his son's coat for warmth, he staggered into the lounge and made such a noise collapsing on the floor that Chris came running. He had an alarmingly high temperature. She started sponging him down. When he passed out she called an ambulance.

Meanwhile Charlie found himself in a tunnel with bright light at the end of it – the classic 'near-death experience'. His mother and grandfather, both dead, were calling to him. What held him back was the strong smell of antiperspirant on his son's coat. 'No,' he said to his mother, 'I'm not ready to come here yet. I want to go back.'

Charlie spent three weeks in hospital with severe blood poisoning but eventually made a full recovery. 'I can't say I saw God himself,' he told me, 'but I had my proof that there's more to life than the here and now.' Charlie made a commitment to Christ while still in hospital. 'The good thing is, having experienced something like that, I can't think I'll ever be able to deny or lose my faith.'

All this happened over 12 years ago. Charlie says his values have changed and God has helped him and Chris through all kinds of family problems and adventures since then.

Are you praying for anyone who can't seem to grasp the relevance Jesus could have to them? Keep praying – and expect the unexpected.

Friday

Two of them were going to a village called Emmaus, about seven miles from Jerusalem . . . talking with each other about everything that had happened . . . Jesus himself came up and walked along with them; but they were kept from recognizing him.

He asked them, 'What are you discussing together as you walk along?'

They stood still, their faces downcast. One of them, named Cleopas, asked him, 'Are you only a visitor to Jerusalem and do not know the things that have happened there in these days?'

'What things?' he asked.

'About Jesus of Nazareth,' they replied. '. . . They crucified him; but we had hoped that he was the one who was going to

redeem Israel . . . Some of our women amazed us . . . Told us
that they had seen a vision of angels, who said he was alive.'

And beginning with Moses and all the Prophets, he explained
to them what was said in all the Scriptures concerning himself.

(Luke 24.13–23, 27)

Do you know Jesus? Cleopas and the other disciple knew him.
They'd followed him around the countryside, spent time with
him, had conversations with him. They'd seen him with their
eyes, touched him maybe, eaten with him, laughed with him,
seen him performing miracles, seen him tired and sad, elated
and angry, compassionate and incisive. They knew him all right.

But they didn't know him. For one thing, they didn't know
his amazing resurrection power. They'd either seen him killed
with their own eyes or heard reports from friends who had.
Mary who appears at the cross in John 19.25 may have been
the wife of this Cleopas (name-spellings vary). Knowing the
end of the story, it's hard for us to imagine how Jesus' followers must have been feeling. But this Emmaus journey account
is detailed enough for us to pick up clues. We can see acute
disappointment, grief beginning to turn to bitterness and traces
of impatient contempt, both for the hysterical women who
thought Jesus was alive, and for the ignorant stranger. We see
a journey away from Jerusalem, away from Jesus and his friends.
And yet . . . Jesus is going with them – behaviour typical of
him. Not forcing anything but gently pursuing those who think
they are running from him, becoming a companion in ordinary things like walking, talking, sharing a meal.

I know Jesus. Sometimes I've felt intimate with him. At
others I've walked away from him, feeling uncomfortable, or
simply wanting to do my own thing. Often I read, perhaps for
the hundredth time, a few words the Bible has to say about
him and realize I don't understand him at all. Sometimes I
pray and read them again and it's almost as though I'd been

blind in that area and my sight has been restored. My journey to know him fully in his resurrection power has a long way to go!

* * *

Sue Varley told me how her journey has led her from faith, to blindness and unbelief and back to faith again. She became a Christian in her mid-teens but, after a great upset when her house group leaders were expelled from church thought, 'Who needs God?' Over the next 20 years she tried hard to convince herself that he didn't exist. Meanwhile she obtained a good maths degree and a career in computing. Later, retraining as a stress manager and hypnotherapist, she ran a small practice from home. But she became sick of the 'Wealth is God' attitude that prevails in the affluent area where she lived with her husband. She had no idea what was missing but, following an envisioning (though not Christian) seminar, was able to let go of some of the long-standing hurt and resentment, and especially the feeling that God had rejected her. Then, on holiday in Scotland, she and her husband decided to uproot from their house and jobs and move to Inverness in search of a better life. I met Sue there at a writing workshop and she explained how their recent move to Scotland had been part of her journey back to God: an extraordinary series of 'coincidences' had helped her find a church where she is now very happy. 'I've been teaching myself wrong things for years and I'm a slow learner but I'm getting to know Jesus again, and letting him change me back to what he always wanted me to be.' Sue was so overwhelmed at God's goodness that someone else had to read out these words that she had written about her journey.

> I set off in the morning with a heart full of hope. The day was new, my life was new, and you were with me. Where would we go, together? What would we see, together? What would I learn from you?

110

I left you early in the journey, I went my own way, I still don't quite know why. I know it hurt, and I was angry, so I ran off alone, so far, so fast, to leave you far behind.

I heard your voice, I felt your call, I said, 'No', 'Go Away', 'Leave Me Alone' and I still did not know why. And I ran on, so far. Slower now, I had no strength, but still I moved away.

But somewhere along the way, the direction changed. I'd gone so far, I was coming back. A long time, moving back, moving slowly, moving closer, not knowing I was going back to you.

And here I am, and here you are, and I won't leave again. Together we'll go on.

I know where I've been, every step of the way, and it wasn't all bad, and I'd go there again to get here. And now I know why, my answer I have is, 'Because'.

Where are you on your journey? Or, perhaps more importantly, in which direction are you facing? How do you see Jesus right now?

Saturday

Half a man

Most of my life, they've called me 'Twin' – my own people in Aramaic and the Gentiles in Greek. I suppose it was the most obvious thing about me. And the next most obvious? That my twin is missing. He died when I was 16. Fishing accident. Small boat, big storm. I lived. He didn't. Before that we each had our own names, but we were always together. We were 'The Twins', then. After he died I felt like half a person, less than half. Couldn't get close to anyone else. If you're a twin you'll understand the intimacy of sharing a womb and a crib, of being together, always, learning to walk, sharing thoughts with little need for speech, fighting sometimes, feeling each other's pain. Closer than husband and wife, some people say.

After my 'other half' died I carried on fishing with the others. We'd grown up together, but when you've been that intimate with someone, everyone else seems a bit . . . distant. I didn't know what they were thinking. They didn't know what I was thinking. I avoided telling them.

And then Jesus came along. Something about him . . . he seemed to know me. Sometimes he said things and it was like this light switched on. Sometimes we used to go fishing at night. We'd go out in the boats and light a lamp. When we held it over the water we could see the tops of the waves – and the fish below rushed into the light, hundreds of them. The water teemed with life. The effect Jesus had on people was a bit like that light; he made everything come alive. But then he'd say something else and I wouldn't get it. He might as well have been talking Egyptian. Mind you, it was the same with all of us who followed him around, seven of us fishing friends and the rest. We gave up our boats to follow him around the country, stayed close to him, thought we were getting to know him and then he'd say something which made no sense to us, made us uneasy – scared too.

Some of them got closer to him. I always felt on the edge, though I would have died for him. He told us he was the Way and I kind of believed him, though I didn't understand. The way we were following seemed very up-and-down, very forward-and-back. He told us he was the resurrection and the life. And then he died. Like my twin died. Only more horribly. And he needn't have died, not Jesus, not then. At the very least he could have stayed away from Jerusalem.

After a few days came rumours of . . . of his resurrection. First from some women, then from my old fishing friends. They said he'd breathed on them. No, it was nothing like a ghost. Warm breath, holy breath, the breath of life. 'Think of God breathing life into Adam!' they told me, their eyes shining. His breathing had brought them alive, truly alive, when they'd not even been dead.

I thought they were dreaming foolish wishes. I, of all people, knew that the dead don't come back to life, however much you miss them. I told them that for a whole week. They were going crazy. I was going crazy. His death had been dreadful enough, but the torture of this ridiculous hope . . . 'No, I don't see! Give me proof, proof that I can touch!' I yelled, feeling more on the outside than ever.

And then, suddenly, there he stood, right in the middle of us, evidently having found a way through locked doors as well as death. He stood there saying, 'Peace!' in his familiar voice. Peace? My mind, everything I thought I knew, had just been blown apart.

He showed me the nail marks in his hands, big ones. 'Come closer, Twin,' he said. 'Put your finger here.' I'd demanded proof of something touchable so I couldn't refuse, but how my hand shook as I obeyed. Then he lifted up his robe and asked me to do something even harder. I sawthe gaping hole in his side where the Roman sword had pierced him to the heart. 'Put your hand in my side, Twin,' he said.

Can you imagine anything more intimate, even for someone who has been a twin? I touched the risen Christ, touched him on the inside. From that moment I've known him not just as a man who shone a light and said amazing, puzzling things. I know him as my Lord and my God, know him in worship and in friendship, know him as the resurrection and the life – know that he really is the way to teeming life for all who come to him.

Astounding that he invited me to touch him in that way. Unique. Changed me utterly. I've travelled far. To Parthia, Persia and further east. You find me here in Edessa. I sense there's not long to go before my resurrection and that of my twin, before we see him again, face to face. I've told so many about him, in Greek and Aramaic, seen him draw close to them, become more intimate than any twin. They know him though they've never seen him with their eyes. I was blind but they see him and he touches them as he touched and touches me. You know what he told me on that astonishing day 30 years ago? 'Blessed are those who have not seen and yet have believed.'

(Imagined from John 20.24–31; 21.2–3; 11.16;
14.3–6 and early church legends)

Spend some intimate moments with Jesus, who alone makes any of us whole.

From suffering and grief to joy

Palm Sunday

To comfort all who mourn . . .
to bestow on them . . .
the oil of gladness
instead of mourning.
(Isaiah 61.2–3)

Would quoting the words above appear tactless to someone in mourning? What about the greeting, 'Happy Easter!' or 'Rejoice in the Lord always. I will say it again: Rejoice!' (Philippians 4.4). These words could sound hearty, heartless even – though faith would affirm that the raw closeness of grief doesn't diminish the joy of Christ's resurrection by one atom.

St Paul also said, 'Rejoice with those who rejoice; mourn with those who mourn' (Romans 12.15) and St Peter, writing at a time when the Church was undergoing persecution: 'Rejoice that you participate in the sufferings of Christ' (1 Peter 4.13).

Gladness and joy are not lightly won . . . or kept. Today is Palm Sunday but Good Friday comes before Easter – and Jesus understands both. Even that old-fashioned word 'merry' (other than in its meaning of 'mildly tipsy') suggests to me Tolkien's Shire, where the good-hearted merriment of ordinary Hobbits had to be (re)won at great price. Suffering at the very least puts gladness into context.

God shows his gentleness as his comfort reaches into the cold bleakness of mourning. Sharp-smelling oils would have been used to anoint bodies for burial but I wonder how the 'oil of gladness' would smell? Warm, with hints of orange perhaps, stimulating the appetite, reaching the subconscious parts of mind and spirit where words can't go? I really don't know, but Isaiah's words suggest to me a soothing massage with this oil, the oil of the Holy Spirit, which seeps, oh so gently, into the cracks and wrinkles, the sore and hidden places, easing joints, softening, smoothing, caressing, healing, bringing comfort and, yes, even bringing gladness.

* * *

On the first Friday of this book I told the story of how Martin Clements' marriage died and came to life again. His wife Joanna related some more of their story.

> In January 1998, a year after Joanna had become a Christian and just a few months after she and Martin began living together again, Joanna became pregnant. She had suffered from pre-eclampsia when expecting their first child, Toby. This time the condition was worse than before and her 20-week scan revealed that it meant the baby wasn't growing properly. Severe anaemia didn't help. Referred to a London hospital, Joanna was told, 'Your baby may well die in the next couple of weeks. If he survives and manages to reach a pound in weight, we can deliver by Caesarean and he might live for up to a year. But he would be badly brain damaged, unable to breathe without oxygen and never out of hospital.' She was told to keep still and do nothing, so that she wouldn't drain any of the vital resources the baby needed.
>
> Joanna remembered the painful days when Toby had lain in intensive care, breathing through a machine. She remembered too how ill she had felt. This time at least she could talk to God about it. Did this baby, did she and Martin, really have to go through all that again – only worse? She prayed that the baby would die.

Her sister-in-law, by contrast, prayed that Joanna would feel the baby move each day. As she began to do so, she and Martin named him Henry. Two weeks later further tests revealed that Henry had died two days previously. They were devastated but also relieved, because he would have been so ill. 'This time, our faith pulled Martin and me through,' Joanna said. 'In fact, through that terrible time, our faith grew. We're not the same people we were before, because we learned beyond doubt that we can trust and depend on God.'

The pregnancy had lasted six months when Joanna delivered Henry's body naturally. They were able to see him and hold him. Then they sent for the hospital chaplain. 'He said afterwards he could tell from our faces that we were Christians,' she said. 'He prayed for moments when we would be able to laugh in our bleakness. At one time those words would have sounded terrible but we knew that Henry had gone back to God. And God himself felt so close, gave us such comfort. I could hear him talking to me.'

Joanna still felt the ache of emptiness of course. Back home, she started stripping paint off their square-shaped banisters – a side a day – and as she did this she'd pray. The day she finished the stairs, she thought, 'What now, God?' And that's when she found out she was pregnant again. This time there were no problems at all: she gave birth to Emma naturally, after a straight-forward six hours of labour.

You might like to meditate on these words from Psalm 139 which have become very special to Joanna:

> Even the darkness will not be dark to you;
> the night will shine like the day,
> for darkness is as light to you.
> For you created my inmost being;
> you knit me together in my mother's womb.
> I praise you because I am fearfully and wonderfully made;

your works are wonderful,
I know that full well.
My frame was not hidden from you
when I was made in the secret place.
When I was woven together in the depths of the earth,
your eyes saw my unformed body.
All the days ordained for me
were written in your book
before one of them came to be.

(Psalm 139.10–16)

Monday

Praise be to the God and Father of our Lord Jesus Christ! In his great mercy he has given us new birth into a living hope through the resurrection of Jesus Christ from the dead, and into an inheritance that can never perish, spoil or fade – kept in heaven for you, who through faith are shielded by God's power until the coming of the salvation that is ready to be revealed in the last time. In this you greatly rejoice, though now for a little while you may have had to suffer grief in all kinds of trials. These have come so that your faith – of greater worth than gold, which perishes even though refined by fire – may be proved genuine and may result in praise, glory and honour when Jesus Christ is revealed. Though you have not seen him, you love him; and even though you do not see him now, you believe in him and are filled with an inexpressible and glorious joy, for you are receiving the goal of your faith, the salvation of your souls.

(1 Peter 1.3–9)

The trouble with passages like this is that they can sound glib. Yet Peter wasn't writing lightly; he knew suffering himself and his readers were undergoing intense persecution. Although rejoicing when you're suffering sounds ridiculous, even on a practical level, it makes sense. If you'll excuse the example, I remember a group of us brand new mums discussing how hard it had become to do something as normal as relieving ourselves. 'Try smiling,' said a friendly nurse, 'it makes the necessary muscles relax!' It worked. A businessman told me he's learned that smiling when making a difficult or contentious phone call also makes a real difference, if only because it helps him appreciate that on the other end of the phone is a real person! The other day, visiting a cancer help centre, I noticed they were running a laughter therapy session. Laughter, said the poster, releases endorphins (the body's natural painkillers), promotes happiness, well-being and health, even exercises our muscles.

On a deeper level, isn't it amazing how some of the best artistic creations and most uplifting thoughts come out of great suffering; how from times of unimaginable evil and degradation, such as the Holocaust, outstanding goodness and courage emerge? Great beauty can shine from the appalling ugliness. If you don't believe me, try reading the exquisite, prize-winning novel *Fugitive Pieces* by Anne Michaels (Bloomsbury, 1998). Only at night can one begin to see the infinity of stars.

Suffering, though, can make us feel so alone. I wrote this poem as I watched a dear friend.

> 'How are you?'
> 'Fine,' she said.
> But I knew that pain
> stabbed her awake,
> dragged dully through her days,
> that worry
> spiralled her brain.
>
> How would she carry
> her children, house, shopping
> . . . her faith, for it
> no longer seemed to carry her?

Even those who knew
didn't always want to hear.
To tell of the pain, yet again
shamed her.
So, 'How are you?'
'Fine,' she said.

Smiles, laughter, even deep wells of human goodness and sympathy are not enough – and Peter was not writing of them. He tells of a supernatural joy coming through the resurrection of his Lord. Christ himself endured all his suffering for the joy of knowing us. Our hope arises from the knowledge that, whatever happens, we will be with him, the one we love above all else.

* * *

Angela Griffiths has experienced far more than her fair share of ill-health and suffering. When people lose their health, a grieving process often sets in. But Angela has found the truth in Peter's words. They have brought hope and joy to her own life. Still not in good health, she spends much of her time encouraging others. I know, because of the way in which she has encouraged me over the years. She told me:

It felt as if I was walking my own way of the cross, in those weeks leading up to Easter. This was some years ago and I had been admitted as an emergency to a large city hospital. Weeks later I was still in hospital. The effects of my illness were devastating and I felt shocked that my normally healthy body had let me down. The most upsetting part was that I was unable to use my hands; they were painful, clawed up and partially paralysed. I couldn't even hold a tissue to wipe away my tears of frustration!

My hands did recover, eventually, and I am thankful for that. I am also profoundly thankful for the hope that kept me buoyant throughout that dark time. The comforting spirit of God brought hope by reminding me of God's faithfulness in the past. Deep down I felt safe because I trusted God. I realize now, it was the same hope that the apostle Peter experienced. In his New Testament letters he refers to the living hope we have through the resurrection of Jesus Christ from the dead. Not a glimmer of hope, but a living hope! With this hope, grounded in the love of God, we are strengthened and encouraged, even in the most difficult circumstances. With this hope we are enabled to accept change.

After my stay in hospital I needed time to adjust. Life went on, although not the same as before. None of us can know what the future holds, but as people of faith we know that we are not alone. We can rejoice because God is with us. His unchanging love sustains our hope.

Pray for any you know who are undergoing an intense time of suffering. Prayer does make a difference!

Tuesday

> God is our refuge and strength,
> an ever-present help in trouble.
> Therefore we will not fear, though the earth give way
> and the mountains fall into the heart of the sea,
> though its waters roar and foam
> and the mountains quake with their surging . . .
> The LORD Almighty is with us;
> the God of Jacob is our fortress . . .
> Be still, and know that I am God;
> I will be exalted among the nations,
> I will be exalted in the earth.
>
> (Psalm 46.1–3, 7, 10)

In September 2003, Hurricane Isobel was threatening the east coast of the USA. Three States and Washington, DC were 'closing down' according to the BBC news. The reporter startled me when he added, 'The time of preparations is past, the time to hope and pray is almost come.'

Some Christians give the impression that their faith guarantees them wealth, health and a trouble-free life. But that's not what we observe in reality and it's not what we read in the Bible. In this Psalm God is described as 'an ever-present help in trouble', which is quite different from his being our own personal trouble-shooter.

When trouble or suffering comes I can spiral down the routes of thinking either that he's not powerful enough to intervene or that he doesn't care, despite all the evidence I've seen to the contrary. I need to enter into the plot and emotions of his story, in which I'm nowhere near a main character! Imagine the Father's love for his Son; and yet he let him suffer before raising him from the dead. But he is God, he will be exalted.

Christians have experienced cataclysms more frightful than earthquakes and tidal waves in the past and will do in the future. Whatever happens, though, God himself promises to be with us. He himself will be our fortress, not cocooning us from all hurt but defending the innermost, eternal parts of us, ensuring that nothing can separate us from him. Life may throw at us pain as disorientating as an earthquake, but as we recognize him at the centre of our lives we find that it's a still centre. The stillness we find in him gives a wholly different rhythm or perspective. We discover a trust in his ultimate power.

* * *

It's terrible when someone you love is terminally ill and in pain. My mother-in-law, Joyce Leonard, told me about an experience she had as her mother was dying.

> Mum wanted to die, at the end. 'Why won't God take me?' she gasped. 'I'm ready to go!' Radiotherapy could do no more for her and we all knew this cancer of the throat was terminal. I

hated to see her suffer like that in hospital. We were so close, I suppose because I was an only child and because she was only 21 years older than me. Back home I broke down and cried. It must have been loud because our neighbour knocked on the door to see if anything was wrong. But I was simply crying to God, 'Why won't you take her?'

And then I had a dream, though I didn't seem to be asleep so perhaps it was a vision. Anyway I seemed to be in heaven and there was this bright light. Not like any other light I've ever seen, which always has a yellowish tinge. This was piercing, dazzling white. I could see a throne and a figure sitting on it, though I wasn't allowed to see the figure properly. Above the throne a great rainbow was shining and above the rainbow the words, 'Be still and know that I am God!'

As I woke up (or came to) my first thought was, I've been with God! And then I realized how appropriate were the words I saw in the dream. Mum died peacefully in her sleep three days later and I was peaceful too. I've never forgotten what I saw – and later I found a passage, in Ezekiel 1.26–8, which described it exactly: 'Above the expanse over their heads was what looked like a throne of sapphire, and high above on the throne was a figure like that of a man . . . brilliant light surrounded him. Like the appearance of a rainbow in the clouds on a rainy day, so was the radiance around him.' I'd never read these verses before and was amazed. Psalm 46 has continued to mean a lot to me as well, 'God is our refuge and strength, an ever-present help in trouble. Therefore we will not fear, though the earth give way . . . Be still and know that I am God.'

Be still and know that he is God.

Wednesday

Therefore put on the full armour of God, so that when the day of evil comes, you may be able to stand your ground, and after you have done everything, to stand. Stand firm then, with the belt of truth buckled round your waist, with the breastplate of righteousness in place, and with your feet fitted with the readiness that comes from the gospel of peace. In addition to all this, take up the shield of faith, with which you can extinguish all the flaming arrows of the evil one. Take the helmet of salvation and the sword of the Spirit, which is the word of God. And pray in the Spirit on all occasions with all kinds of prayers and requests. With this in mind, be alert and always keep on praying for all the saints.   (Ephesians 6.13–18)

The Bible is nothing if not practical. At times when I've known suffering or been crushed, I haven't felt in the least as though I was advancing in my Christian faith. All I could do was to stand. But those are the very times when it's proved that we're not alone and defenceless. Paul's words suggest that we have do something first, something easy, though it appears difficult. It reminds me a bit of relaxing during childbirth. That's what they tell you to do in antenatal classes: when the contractions come, relax and breathe. It sounds simple – anyone can relax, anyone can breathe. But I guess our natural reaction to pain is to tense up, to prepare for flight or fight: relaxing is counter-intuitive. I soon found in labour, though, that if I did as I was told – relax, breathe and let the waves of pain wash over me without fighting them – I could bear it. If I tensed up, well, it was so dreadful I didn't do it much!

Dressing up in Roman-style armour sounds simple though quaint, not something to bother with when *in extremis*. But it's about changing our attitude, changing everything. For we do have a belt of truth to hold us together when we're sagging in the middle. It's the truth that Jesus loves us, whatever we feel. Should we feel we've let him down, he hands us the breastplate of his righteousness. We find enough of a shield of faith in him to ward off thoughts which, when we are suffering or crushed, really can come like fiery arrows. Such thoughts singe us painfully with despair or bitterness or even catch light, burning up our very selves. The helmet of salvation, jammed over our sometimes thick heads, reminds us that, whatever happens, God is strong to save. We can even begin to wield the sword of the Spirit and find, as Jesus did, that God's words put paid to temptation and fear, strengthening us where we're weak. Now we can pray, beyond our minds, in his Spirit.

* * *

I find Paul's picture-language helpful, though soldiers, armour and battles aren't my favourite imagery. The truth that God helps us to 'stand' in difficult places was illustrated in a different way when I was leading a writing workshop in Scotland on the theme of valleys. Mary Bisset finished her assignment early and came to talk to me.

> 'We went through quite a valley last year,' she said. 'At the time friends said they didn't know how I was coping. I was surprised too – but God made it lighter somehow. He gave me strength and hope in ways I wouldn't have believed possible. He really was with us in that valley.'

Mary told me that her twin sons were everything to her, so when doctors diagnosed one of them with an extremely rare form of leukaemia it came as a terrible shock. Her husband was away, working on an oil rig. But Mary and her 14-year-old son Steven both had a living faith. Soon people all over the world were praying. Steven's bones were already 'moth-eaten' as chemotherapy began. To watch her son go through that treatment was horrible, especially as it had to happen 200 miles from home, but God was there, helping them through. When downhearted one day, Mary asked for a song in her spirit and then wondered why she was singing inside. As she held Steven's hands while yet again the doctor tried to drain fluid from his lung, she asked, 'God, why do I have to see my son suffer like this?' In a flash, she saw the cross. Nails had pierced Jesus' body, not a needle, but she knew that Father God understood her pain. Another time when Steven was extremely ill, Mary heard strange mutterings and thought he was hallucinating. Then, kneeling close by his bedside she understood the words. He was putting on God's armour. 'A 14-year-old,' she exclaimed, 'showing me what to do!'

When their first attempt at a second kind of chemotherapy successfully removed the cancerous cells one doctor said it was nothing short of a miracle. Then came the question of finding the right match for a bone marrow transplant. 'Perhaps that's why God gave us twins!' said Mary. After eight months they were able to return home. Was this the end, Mary found herself asking God? Then she picked up a magazine and read a head-line, 'It is finished.'

Ten weeks later Steven was riding an All Terrain Vehicle in a field eight feet above the road near his house. He hit an embankment, soared further into the air and crashed a total of 15 feet down on to the road below, narrowly missing some iron railings. He had jumped clear of the ATV. It hit a moving jeep and split in two. One half of it damaged a parked car.

A neighbour saw it all happen, but Mary was in the shower, preparing to go to the cinema. While waiting for the ambu-lance, Mary cradled Steven's head and couldn't help thinking of the title of the James Bond film they would now miss – *Die Another Day*.

Steven wasn't dead but one of his knees was broken, the other cracked; he'd broken his toe and both wrists, one so severely that the doctor said he'd never seen anything like it. He would try to reset it, but it would probably need pins and wires which, because of Steven's medical history, was too complex a pro-cedure for that hospital. Again, Mary got people praying. Less than three weeks later the casts were removed for examination. When Steven began to wriggle his wrist the doctors could hardly believe it – no way should it have mended so fast. They didn't even need to reapply the plaster.

Musing on their journey through the dark valley, Mary highlighted words which came to missionary Dr Helen Roseveare while praying: 'Can you thank me for trusting you with this experience, even if I never tell you why?'

Give me what I need to stand before you, Father God, in good times and in bad.

Thursday

Jesus . . . said to them, 'Are you asking one another what I meant when I said, "In a little while you will see me no more, and then after a little while you will see me?" I tell you the truth, you will weep and mourn while the world rejoices. You will grieve, but your grief will turn to joy. A woman giving birth to a child has pain because her time has come; but when her baby is born she forgets the anguish because of her joy that a child is born into the world. So with you: Now is your time of grief, but I will see you again and you will rejoice, and no one will take away your joy.   (John 16.19–22)

We have the advantage of knowing that the disciples' grief at the death of Jesus would turn, just a few days later in Jerusalem, to joy beyond words. Jesus had told them they were destined for both great suffering and great joy. In the same discourse with his disciples, John records him as saying,

'It is for your good that I am going away. Unless I go away, the Counsellor will not come to you; but if I go, I will send him to you . . . he will guide you into all truth. He will not speak on his own; he will speak only what he hears, and he will tell you what is yet to come . . . He will bring glory to me by taking from what is mine and making it known to you.   (John 16.7, 13–14)

But Jesus has also just said, 'They will put you out of the synagogue; in fact, a time is coming when anyone who kills you will think he is offering a service to God.'

Mary's labour pains as she gave birth to God's Son were short compared to the labour pains of the birth of his Kingdom, which have lasted, so far, over 2,000 years. But unlike giving birth to a human being, which is only over when a mother holds her warm, wriggling, bawling babe in her arms, we have joy along the way. Jesus is risen, alive, interceding for us, the Holy Spirit is with us, closer than breathing. Our suffering and sacrifices aren't yet over but, meanwhile, no one can separate us from God's love.

* * *

Pam Conolly's pastor set the church creative team an assignment: if it were possible for us to kiss God, what in practical terms would that entail? Pam expressed her answer through the poem below. 'It's the point at which our half-hearted, feeble attempts in seeking God give way to total self-abandonment and the kind of aggressive, unbridled, passionate worship that breaks through every pain barrier and limitation in hungry pursuit of him,' she told me. Her poem reminds me of the pain and joys of giving birth. You might like to pray it for yourself.

The kiss
When all I have and all I am,
my deepest longings, dreams and plans,
all my hopes and aspirations,
my wildest expectations,
each proud and lofty thought
every empire I have built . . .

the things that bring me pleasure,
the most sacred of my treasures,

all my talents and my gifts,
my essence and my strength,
my every moment, every breath . . .
lie surrendered, discarded, abandoned at his feet . . .

When my steady pulse starts racing,
gentle tremors turn to shaking,
my reaching becomes straining,
and I'm pushing through the pain . . .
when my longing turns to aching,
my yielding becomes breaking
and the torrent of my tears
can no longer be restrained . . .

when wanting's feeble moan
gives way to hunger's growling groan
and night and day I'm calling out his name . . .

when passion's raging fire
consumes the flicker of desire
and dying embers burst into a flame . . .

somewhere in the midst
there's a moment of pure bliss
when Earth connects with heaven
and God receives my kiss!

Good Friday

But when they came to Jesus and found that he was already
dead, they did not break his legs. Instead, one of the soldiers
pierced Jesus' side with a spear, bringing a sudden flow of blood
and water. The man who saw it has given testimony, and his
testimony is true. He knows that he tells the truth, and he testi-
fies so that you also may believe. These things happened so that
the scripture would be fulfilled: 'Not one of his bones will be
broken,' and, as another scripture says, 'They will look on the
one they have pierced.'   (John 19.33–7)

The other day I switched on the television in the middle of an interview with the Welsh bass-baritone, Bryn Terfel. As he chatted pleasantly about his country and his music, in the background, a graphic oil painting depicted Christ's broken body being carried away from the cross. The fact that no one referred to it while we were watching gave me a jolt, making me realize how unshocking the crucifixion appears to me normally. I've become over-familiar with this terrible event at the heart of everything. Our church prayers and worship rightly centre around it, but constant repetition can cushion us from reality.

However could joy and hope come from the torture of God's Son – the one who was there at the creation of everything? His mental and spiritual agony must have been even greater than the physical pain. You would think that his extreme suffering gave grounds for extreme grief at the hopelessness of cruel humanity – and so for the obliterating anger of God. Why didn't that happen? Today's verses from John's Gospel give a number of clues 'for those with eyes to see'. Blood and water flowing from the wound on Jesus' side meant, on a physical level, that his heart was pierced: he was certainly dead. To the Jews blood meant sacrifice and a bridge back to God; it meant life poured out; it meant a committed, covenant relationship. Water in that dry land meant God's abundant provision; it meant life and cleansing, healing grace.

The original readers would also have been familiar with John's scriptural allusions. The first quotation is from Psalm 34: 'The LORD is close to the broken-hearted and saves those who are crushed in spirit. A righteous man may have many troubles, but the LORD delivers him from them all; he protects all his bones, not one of them will be broken.' Jesus, the righteous one, is given the power to save – all the more because his own heart was broken.

The second quotation refers to Zechariah 12.10 and 13.1:

'I will pour out on the house of David and the inhabitants of Jerusalem a spirit of grace and supplication. They will look on me, the one they have pierced, and they will mourn for him as one mourns for an only child, and grieve bitterly for him as one grieves for a firstborn son . . . On that day a fountain will be opened to the house of David and the inhabitants of Jerusalem, to cleanse them from sin and impurity.'

It is by acknowledging and mourning for the terrible things that we have done, to each other and to God, that we can find right relationships with both again. The mourners will be comforted. Appreciating the weight of the cross is necessary before we can know the joy of the resurrection.

* * *

Caroline Lovejoy works for the Shaftesbury Society as Assistant Director of Adult Support, delivering 'Whole Life' services for people with learning and physical disabilities. Here she writes about her first childhood experience of mourning.

I wept. The sobbing wouldn't stop. I gasped and gulped. Tears ran down my cheeks and dripped off my chin and even in the midst of my grief I saw they splashed dark jagged circles on my red shoes. He was dead. The grown-ups didn't know what to do and patted me like a dog and said it would be all right. But I knew they lied.

I trailed home. I didn't care who saw. I jabbed a stick in the ground, but it broke. I hated the bright yellow flowers and wanted to stomp on them all, but I didn't dare.

He is dead. Life is no more. He is gone. No more laughing in the dragonfly meadow. No more looking at the moon in a puddle. No more running home from school to tell him the stories of the day, to show him my pictures. No more sharing of a cut finger or a new friend with blue velvet ribbons. It's not fair. In the whole wide world it was the worsest possible thing.

Mummy doesn't care or doesn't see or doesn't know. She is a long way off. Anyroad it won't go into little word-shapes. It's too big and too horrid. I am all alone now. No one can touch me in this place. The hurt is bigger than me. It hurts worse than a scraped shin, but there's no scrape to mend.

No one thought to tell me that he didn't die for ever, that three days later he is risen. The grown-ups were blasé at the death of Jesus because they knew, far too well, he'd be back on Sunday.

Help us all to understand a little more of what you did, Jesus.

Easter Saturday

Three scenes for Mary

1   It's dark and I cannot sleep. It's cold and I cannot rest; so tired but I can't keep still. Yet how can I think about me when that sight, those sounds, that smell have obliterated everything? I'm nothing now, a shadow in the sleeping streets where the dogs bark. Someone snores and someone screams.

The others said I risked too much by going there, so I slipped out alone. It's their choice. I would not put their lives in danger, but what does it matter now what the soldiers do to me?

I'm aware it's useless. I won't even see that poor, battered body, what with the guards and the stone and the linen cloths. Those high-ups, the one from the Sanhedrin and the rich one, they tried to make it 'all right'. I suppose I would have done the same, had they let me – tried to bandage his body though it was infinitely beyond repair, covering those obscene wounds, that fleshless back as though this was a normal death. But not even their hundred pounds of myrrh and aloes can smother the stench of what's been done.

Ironic when I, in my way, also anointed his body with precious perfume. What good did that do? They say magi brought myrrh to him at his mother's breast. Did they, did I without knowing it, foretell this ... desolation then? For what? We believed in him, all of us, we loved him. I loved him, he loved me. I touched his feet with my fingers, my lips; and though I wiped the perfume from them with my hair he did not push me away. How could they mutilate those feet? Cold, sterile, wiped clean of blood and rust, they'll smell of overpowering perfume now, not of himself. All that life, all that promise, all that hope he gave us, frozen, stiff, decayed, gone.

2   You wouldn't think I could cry any more yet the tears keep dropping like acid from my eyes and those are my sobs echoing in the stone chamber. It's dawn now but I can't see the new day. I imagined things couldn't get worse, that I couldn't understand less but ... no soldiers, no stone seal, no body. They could have left us that. For me time wouldn't have healed; even after years I would never have been able to lay the stones calmly at his tomb according to our custom, not after all he meant, all he did for me. Perhaps, for some of the others ... Peter and John have come – I ran to find them but my feet won't move now. These men, his two friends, have gone again. I don't know where to go. I don't know what to do, not just for this hour but for the rest of my life.

3   He has gone again but I am dancing, leaping, running. The sun is rising in the sky but it is not as bright as he, the Son of God, the Son of Man. I've seen his savaged, holed body more whole, more alive than anyone's ever was, ever could be. And still he loves me; he spoke my name. How can it be that I, called a prostitute, a woman disgraced, am the first human being to see such a one alive? Yet I still live myself! I touched him. And of course I understand now. 'Don't hold me,' he said. Of course I

133

can't hold him any more than I could hold the sun. I must tell
the others. He IS. He IS for all of us. He is the life that is in us. He
was crushed in order to give us this wine; the dark came but now
the light is here and nothing will be the same again.

> (Imagined from the Bible passion and
> resurrection narratives)

May I know the joy of your power and love rising in me, risen
Lord.

Death to new life

Easter Sunday

On the shore

I woke in the middle of the night and he'd gone. Had he spent the night on the lake, just like in the old days? That's why I ran down there at first light, sheltered from the wind behind a boat, watching, hoping. And there they were – James, John, Nathanael, the one they call 'The Twin', my man and a couple of others I didn't recognize – in the old boat, sailing back to shore. Judging by where the boat sat in the water, they hadn't caught much. Probably forgotten how, after all this time, I thought. But at least they had the boat back in the water, working. At least they hadn't sunk. Perhaps life would become bearable again for me, Mum, the kids. Have you any idea what it's like for a husband to up and off with some wandering nutter? I don't mean for a few days. I mean months, years.

That's what I thought, that morning, before I smelt fish cooking on the beach and noticed the stranger tending a charcoal fire. 'Course I had no idea it was him. Well, would you expect to find a dead person calmly cooking fish? You know, I was glad when he died! Not the way of it – that was horrible. I wouldn't wish it on anybody. But he'd taken my Simon away, that's what I thought. And now Simon, my husband, was back. Depressed, but back. As I say, I had hoped that things would return to normal.

Normal! Just a few years after that morning on the lake shore and I'm married not to a village fisherman but to someone in charge of a movement that's taking the mighty Roman Empire by storm. A man who touches people and they're healed, a man who walked out of chains, out of prison, a man who preached to huge crowds of people – foreigners – and they all understood him. That's 'normal' life now – bigger, brighter, bolder and more dangerous than I could have imagined. You know what the risen Jesus promised my husband that day after he'd told the men where to catch more fish than any of us could possibly eat? He said that when Simon was old he would be killed, just as Jesus was killed, to glorify God. How do I feel about all this? I struggle. Wouldn't you? But I wouldn't go back to the old life now – not for anything!

(Imagined from John 21)

Rejoice this Easter and count the cost of this new life.

Easter-spirit
The lake, brown or drizzle-
dimpled in muted colours
reflects a graveyard where
daffodils shine brighter
than in sunlight,
and in the little church
they smell sweeter than the rain.

Easter Monday

They will rebuild the ancient ruins
and restore the places long devastated;
they will renew the ruined cities
that have been devastated for generations.
(Isaiah 61.4)

Jesus' resurrection is amazing, but the story goes on. Luke, at the start of Acts, says, 'In my former book (that is, his Gospel)

136

I wrote about all that Jesus began to do and teach until the day he was taken up into heaven.'

In 2,000 years there have been many big stories which entered the history books and still affect all of our lives. Some terrible things have been done in God's name. But think for a moment what the world would be like without Christians who have fought down the ages for righteousness, justice, compassion and peace.

What impresses me most are the countless 'small stories'. Not small in God's eyes: I'm sure he records them even if they never hit the media. So many 'ordinary' individuals do the extraordinary things which God is asking of them, quietly, in his strength. The Spirit of the Lord rests upon 'ordinary' Christians as they draw near to damage and devastation, restoring, building up, loving, believing, bringing new life to what appears to be dried up, dead, useless. Who knows what ripples that causes?

* * *

I've been privileged to hear so many stories of Easter hope for this book. Here's one which sums it all up, really. Tom and Kate Davonport had three children of their own, but their son David was killed in a road accident when he was 17. 'God was faithful through that terrible time,' Kate told me, 'and I have to say it changed us all – changed our priorities so much.' Some ten years later, the couple fostered another child. Here Kate writes a little bit of Emily's story.

Tom and I looked at the little girl and felt a surge of compassion for this helpless, profoundly handicapped child. She was a year old, but she appeared like a newborn babe. We looked at each other with tears in our eyes. We had asked God for a gut reaction to decide whether we should foster her. Jean, the temporary foster mother, looked at us and said, 'You are taking her, aren't you?' We could only nod. Jean said, 'Please can I ask you if you are believing Christians?' We said, 'Yes, we are.' Jean began to cry and told us that their fellowship had been praying for a Christian couple to take Emily long term.

Many friends were concerned about what we were doing, but we had that peace of knowing that we were within God's will in caring for Emily.

Emily came to live with our family and she crept into our hearts. Love blossomed between us. She touched the lives of all who knew her with something special.

The health problems didn't improve and Emily remained as helpless as a baby, but we cared for her with gladness. There was never a moment of regret.

After two years the opportunity came for us to become Emily's legal custodians. After meeting with a social services legal adviser we were advised to adopt. We felt God directing us. Although we were over the age of adopting we went ahead.

This was to take a long time. The social worker, Pam, who had by now become a friend, came to see me. She said very kindly, 'Kate, you and Tom have this vision but it will take a miracle for this adoption to happen.' I felt so deflated. When Pam had gone I went to my daily reading and opened the book. The reading for that day, from Habakkuk 2.3, was, 'The vision is for the appointed time . . . Though it tarries, wait for it, because it will surely come.' I was thrilled. Pam had used that very word 'vision'. We held on to that promise and in 1990 the adoption went through. Emily was our little girl. What joy!

Emily bore countless operations and infections with serenity and then, when she had been with us for 12 years, she died suddenly. This left a huge gap in our lives. Some people thought that the death of an adopted child couldn't feel as bad as that of a natural child. Not true. One death was as crushing as the other, because Emily had become truly ours. But we had peace with the pain in knowing that with Jesus, Emily is now whole.

That there were 300 people at Emily's funeral speaks of the impact one vulnerable little girl had in their lives. Out of her bruised, seemingly pointless life, God gave so many blessings.

Thank you for faith, Lord, and for people of faith. Thank you for hope and for people who bring it. Thank you most of all for love, divine and human. All of these things begin and end in you, eternally.

And now that Easter is past, may we lean towards Whitsun – towards the warm flowering of summer. As we live in your Spirit and dream your dreams, may you breathe through our human voices to give hope to individuals and nations.

The Society for Promoting Christian Knowledge (SPCK) was founded in 1698. Its mission statement is:

To promote Christian knowledge by

- **Communicating the Christian faith in its rich diversity;**

- **Helping people to understand the Christian faith and to develop their personal faith; and**

- **Equipping Christians for mission and ministry.**

SPCK Worldwide serves the Church through Christian literature and communication projects in over 100 countries, and provides books for those training for ministry in many parts of the developing world. This worldwide service depends upon the generosity of others and all gifts are spent wholly on ministry programmes, without deductions.

SPCK Bookshops support the life of the Christian community by making available a full range of Christian literature and other resources, providing support for those training for ministry, and assisting bookstalls and book agents throughout the UK.

SPCK Publishing produces Christian books and resources, covering a wide range of inspirational, pastoral, practical and academic subjects. Authors are drawn from many different Christian traditions, and publications aim to meet the needs of a wide variety of readers in the UK and throughout the world.

The Society does not necessarily endorse the individual views contained in its publications, but hopes they stimulate readers to think about and further develop their Christian faith.

For further information about the Society, visit our website at *www.spck.org.uk* or write to:
SPCK, 36 Causton Street,
London SW1P 4ST, United Kingdom.